D1716604

WELCOME

Thanks for purchasing these training notes for the **AWS Certified Cloud Practitioner** exam from <u>Digital Cloud Training</u>. The information in these Cheat Sheets relates to the latest version of the **CLF-C01** version of the exam blueprint.

The aim of putting this exam-specific information together into one document is to provide a centralized, detailed list of the facts you need to know before you sit your exam. This will shortcut your study time and maximize your chances of passing the AWS Certified Cloud Practitioner exam the first time.

I trust that you'll get great value from this popular resource that has been well received by our pool of over 750,000 students. Through diligent study of these learning materials, you will be in the perfect position to ace your AWS Certified Cloud Practitioner exam with confidence.

Wishing you the best for every step in your cloud journey!

Neal Davis

Founder of Digital Cloud Training

ABOUT THESE TRAINING NOTES

Please note that this document does not read like a book or instructional text. We provide a raw, point-to-point list of facts backed by tables and diagrams to help with understanding.

For easy navigation, the information on each AWS service in this document is organized into the same categories as in the AWS Management Console.

The scope of coverage of services, and what information is included for each service, is based on feedback from our pool of over 750,000 students who have taken the exam, as well as our own experience.

To test your understanding, we have added **120 unique quiz questions** that you will find at the end of each major chapters. Please note that quiz questions are designed as a tool to review your knowledge of the content that was presented within the section. They do <u>not</u> necessarily represent the AWS exam style or difficulty. You will find examples of exam style practice questions within the chapter "<u>How to best prepare for your exam</u>".

WHAT DO OTHER STUDENTS SAY?

Check out the excellent reviews from our many students who passed their AWS exam with an average passing score of over 850!

* * * * *

If I had only known how valuable this book would be, I would've bought this and saved a lot of time and money spent on other sources of AWS study materials. This book provides the AWS Cloud Practitioner Exam content in an organized, easier to understand format for us novice cloudies. Highly recommend.

* * * * *

I enjoyed the book; it was an easy read and a great way to prepare for the Cloud Practitioner exam. Neal Davis explains the concepts clearly, includes great visuals and practice questions. The purchase also gives you the ability to create a Digital Cloud account which provides additional resources (free and paid) including more notes and practice questions and exams.

* * * * *

A must-have study resource for the AWS Certified Cloud Practitioner CLF-C01 exam

TABLE OF CONTENTS

© 2023 Digital Cloud Training

GETTING STARTED

YOUR PATHWAY TO SUCCESS

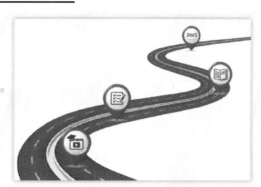

⊘ Enroll in Instructor-led Video Course
Familiarize yourself with the AWS platform

⊘ Take our AWS Practice Exams
Identify your strengths and weaknesses and assess your exam readiness

⊘ Study Training Notes
Focus your study on the knowledge areas where you need to most

⊘ Get AWS Certified
This pathway will let you pass your AWS exam first time with confidence

So, you're feeling excited to get started with the AWS Certified Cloud Practitioner certification and wondering what resources are out there to help you. Let's start with the free options. Visit https://digitalcloud.training/free-aws-certification-training/ for links to various free resources including sample practice questions, blog articles and video tutorials.

For the full training experience though, your best bet are the following training courses:

STEP 1: ON-DEMAND VIDEO COURSE

To get you started, we'd suggest first enrolling in the instructor-led AWS Certified Cloud Practitioner Video Course from Digital Cloud Training to familiarize yourself with the AWS platform before returning to the Training Notes to get a more detailed understanding of the AWS services.

To learn more, visit https://digitalcloud.training/aws-certified-cloud-practitioner/

STEP 2: PRACTICE EXAM COURSE

To assess where you are at on your AWS journey, we recommend taking the AWS Certified Cloud Practitioner Practice Exams on the Digital Cloud Training website. The **online exam simulator** with over **500 unique questions** will help you identify your strengths and weaknesses. These practice tests are designed to reflect the difficulty of the AWS exam and are the closest to the real exam experience available.

To learn more, visit https://digitalcloud.training/aws-certified-cloud-practitioner/

Our online Practice Exams are delivered in 4 different variations:

- **Exam Mode**

  In exam simulation mode, you complete one full-length practice exam and answer all 65 questions within the allotted time. You are then presented with a pass / fail score report showing your overall score and performance in each knowledge area to identify your strengths and weaknesses.

- **Training Mode**

When taking the practice exam in training mode, you will be shown the answers and explanations for every question after clicking "check". Upon completion of the exam, the score report will show your overall score and performance in each knowledge area.

- **Knowledge Reviews**

  Now that you have identified your strengths and weaknesses, you get to dive deep into specific areas with our knowledge reviews. You are presented with a series of questions focused on a specific topic. There is no time limit, and you can view the answer to each question as you go through them.

- **Final Exam Simulator**

  The exam simulator randomly selects 65 questions from our pool of questions – mimicking the real AWS exam environment. The practice exam has the same format, style, time limit and passing score as the real AWS exam

STEP 3: TRAINING NOTES

As a final step, use these training notes to focus your study on the knowledge areas where you need to most. Get a detailed understanding of the AWS services and deep dive into the CLF-C01 exam objectives with detailed facts, tables and diagrams that will shortcut your time to success.

LIMITED TIME BONUS OFFER

To assess your AWS exam readiness, we have included one full-length practice exam from Digital Cloud Training with 65 exam-difficulty practice questions that are timed and scored and simulate the real AWS exam experience. To gain access to your free practice test on our interactive exam simulator online, simply navigate to the CONCLUSION at the back of this book where you'll find detailed instructions.

REQUEST YOUR FREE PDF VERSION OF THIS BOOK

Based on the feedback we've received from our Amazon clients, we understand that studying complex diagrams in black and white or accessing reference links from a kindle device may NOT offer the best learning experience.

That's why we've decided to provide you with a PDF version of this book at **no additional charge**. Simply navigate to the CONCLUSION of this book for instructions on how to access your free PDF version.

CONTACT, SUPPORT & FEEDBACK

We want you to get great value from these training resources. If for any reason you are not 100% satisfied, please contact us at support@digitalcloud.training. We promise to address all questions and concerns, typically within 24hrs. We really want you to have a 5-star learning experience!

The AWS platform is evolving quickly, and the exam tracks these changes with a typical lag of around 6 months. We are therefore reliant on student feedback to keep track of what is appearing in the exam. If there are any topics in your exam that weren't covered in our training resources, please provide us with feedback using this form https://digitalcloud.training/student-feedback/. We appreciate any feedback that will help us further improve our AWS training resources.

REVIEWS REALLY MATTER

If you enjoy reading reviews, please consider paying it forward. Reviews guide students and help us continuously improve our courses. We celebrate every honest review and truly appreciate it. We'd be thrilled if you could leave a rating at amazon.com/ryp or your local amazon store (e.g. amazon.co.uk/ryp).

JOIN THE AWS COMMUNITY

Our private Facebook group is a great place to ask questions and share knowledge and exam tips with the AWS community. Join the AWS Certification QA group on Facebook and share your exam feedback with the AWS community: https://www.facebook.com/groups/awscertificationqa

To join the discussion about all things related to Amazon Web Services on Slack, visit: http://digitalcloud.training/slack for instructions.

CONNECT WITH NEAL ON SOCIAL MEDIA

To learn more about the different ways of connecting with Neal, visit: https://digitalcloud.training/neal-davis

 digitalcloud.training/neal-davis

 youtube.com/c/digitalcloudtraining

 facebook.com/digitalcloudtraining

 Twitter @nealkdavis

 linkedin.com/in/nealkdavis

 Instagram @digitalcloudtraining

HOW TO BEST PREPARE FOR YOUR EXAM

THE AWS EXAM BLUEPRINT

As a foundational level exam, the AWS Certified Cloud Practitioner is intended for individuals who have the ability to, in Amazon's words, "effectively demonstrate an overall understanding of the AWS Cloud". This certification is fairly generic and does not assess the skills required for specific job roles such as Developers, Sysops Administrators and Solutions Architects.

AWS recommend you have a minimum of 6 months experience with the AWS Cloud. However, this does not need to be experience in a technical job role. Exposure to the AWS Cloud in a managerial, sales, purchasing or financial position is also acceptable.

The exam includes 65 questions and has a time limit of 90 minutes. You need to score a minimum of 700 out of 1000 points to pass the exam.

The question format of the exam is multiple-choice (one correct response from four options) and multiple-response (two correct responses from five options).

As you'll see from the example questions later in this chapter, the questions are fairly straightforward and <u>not</u> scenario based like in other exams such as the Associate and Professional level certifications.

In the AWS Certified Cloud Practitioner exam blueprint, it is stated that **the exam validates an examinee's ability to**:

- Define what the AWS Cloud is and the basic global infrastructure
- Describe basic AWS Cloud architectural principles
- Describe the AWS Cloud value proposition
- Describe key services on the AWS platform and their common use cases (for example, compute and analytics)
- Describe basic security and compliance aspects of the AWS platform and the shared security model
- Define the billing, account management and pricing models
- Identify sources of documentation or technical assistance (for example, whitepapers or support tickets)
- Describe basic/core characteristics of deploying and operating in the AWS Cloud

Throughout the rest of this chapter, we'll explore these knowledge requirements in more detail, and will give you a clear idea of what to expect in the exam.

DOMAINS, OBJECTIVES AND EXAMPLES

The knowledge required is organized into four test "domains". Within each test domain there are several objectives that broadly describe the knowledge and experience expected to pass the exam.

Test Domain 1: Cloud Concepts

This domain makes up 28% of the exam and includes the following three objectives:

- 1.1 Define the AWS Cloud and its value proposition
- 1.2 Identify aspects of AWS Cloud economics
- 1.3 List the different cloud architecture design principles

What you need to know

You should be able to describe the benefits of public cloud services and be able to define what types of services are available on AWS (think IaaS, PaaS, SaaS). Make sure you understand the 6 advantages of cloud:

1. Trade capital expense for variable expense
2. Benefit from massive economies of scale
3. Stop guessing about capacity
4. Increase speed and agility
5. Stop spending money running and maintaining data centers
6. Go global in minutes

You need to know how cloud is beneficial from a financial perspective and should understand the difference between CAPEX and OPEX – this relates to item 1 in the list above.

You should understand the design principles of creating cloud architectures, this includes loose coupling, scaling (vertically and horizontally), bootstrapping and automation, to name just a few.

Example questions

Question: *Which feature of AWS allows you to deploy a new application for which the requirements may change over time?*

1. Elasticity
2. Fault tolerance
3. Disposable resources
4. High availability

Answer: 1, elasticity allows you to deploy your application without worrying about whether it will need more or less resources in the future. With elasticity, the infrastructure can scale on-demand

Question: *What advantages do you get from using the AWS cloud? (choose 2)*

1. Trade capital expense for variable expense
2. Stop guessing about capacity
3. Increased capital expenditure
4. Gain greater control of the infrastructure layer
5. Comply with all local security compliance programs

Answer: 1+2, with public cloud services such as AWS you can pay on a variable (OPEX) basis for the resources you use and scale on-demand, so you never need to guess how much resources you need to deploy.

Test Domain 2: Security

This domain makes up 24% of the exam and includes the following four objectives:

- 2.1 Define the AWS Shared Responsibility mode
- 2.2 Define AWS Cloud security and compliance concepts
- 2.3 Identify AWS access management capabilities
- 2.4 Identify resources for security support

What you need to know

You should understand the AWS shared responsibility model which defines who is responsible for different aspects of the technology stack from the data center through to servers, firewall rules and data encryption.

AWS provide tools and services for implementing security, assessing your security position, and generating alerts and compliance reports. You need to understand these services and tools well enough to describe their usage and benefits. This includes services such as KMS, CloudTrail and AWS Artifact.

You also need to understand the services that are used for authentication, authorization and access management. This includes services such as AWS IAM, and Amazon Cognito, and the usage of access keys, key pairs and signed URLs.

Support services include real-time insights through AWS Trusted Advisor and proactive support and advocacy with a Technical Account Manager (TAM). Make sure you know which support packages include a TAM.

Example questions

Question: *Under the AWS shared responsibility model what is the customer responsible for? (choose 2)*

1. Physical security of the data center
2. Replacement and disposal of disk drives
3. Configuration of security groups
4. Patch management of infrastructure
5. Encryption of customer data

Answer: 3+5, AWS are responsible for items such as the physical security of the DC, replacement of old disk drives, and patch management of the infrastructure whereas customers are responsible for items such as configuring security groups, network ACLs, patching their operating systems and encrypting their data.

Question: *Which AWS service is used to enable multi-factor authentication?*

1. Amazon STS
2. AWS IAM
3. Amazon EC2
4. AWS KMS

Answer: 2, IAM is used to securely control individual and group access to AWS resources and can be used to manage multi-factor authentication.

Test Domain 3: Technology

This domain makes up 36% of the exam and includes the following four objectives:

- 3.1 Define methods of deploying and operating in the AWS Cloud
- 3.2 Define the AWS global infrastructure
- 3.3 Identify the core AWS services
- 3.4 Identify resources for technology support

What you need to know

You need to understand the core AWS services and what they are used for. You typically don't need a deep level of knowledge of the specifics of a service but do need to understand its purpose, benefits and use cases.

Core services include EC2, ECS, Lambda, LightSail, EBS, EFS, S3, RDS, DynamoDB, RedShift, ElastiCache, Elastic Load Balancing, Auto Scaling, CloudFront, Route 53, CloudWatch, CloudTrail, and SNS.

You should understand the underlying global infrastructure that makes up the AWS Cloud. This includes regions, availability zones, and edge locations. Make sure you understand which services are globally or regionally defined.

You should also know the customer configurable building blocks of cloud services including VPCs, and subnets, and connectivity options such as Internet Gateways, VPN and Direct Connect. Also, ensure you know the difference between NAT Instances and NAT Gateways and the relative benefits of each service.

Example questions

Question: *What are the advantages of Availability Zones? (choose 2)*

1. They allow regional disaster recovery
2. They provide fault isolation
3. They enable the caching of data for faster delivery to end users
4. They are connected by low-latency network connections
5. They enable you to connect your on-premises networks to AWS to form a hybrid cloud

Answer: 2+4, Each AWS region contains multiple distinct locations called Availability Zones (AZs). Each AZ is engineered to be isolated from failures in other AZs. An AZ is a data center, and in some cases, an AZ consists of multiple data centers. AZs within a region provide inexpensive, low-latency network connectivity to other zones in the same region. This allows you to replicate your data across data centers in a synchronous manner so that failover can be automated and be transparent for your users.

Question: *Which AWS support plans provide support via email, chat and phone? (choose 2)*

1. Basic

2. Business
3. Developer
4. Global
5. Enterprise

Answer: 2+5, only the business and enterprise plans provide support via email, chat and phone.

Test Domain 4: Billing and Pricing

This domain makes up 12% of the exam and includes the following three objectives:

- 4.1 Compare and contrast the various pricing models for AWS
- 4.2 Recognize the various account structures in relation to AWS billing and pricing
- 4.3 Identify resources available for billing support

What you need to know

Most services on AWS are offered on a pay per use basis, but there are also options to reduce price by locking in to 1- or 3-year contracts with various options for payment. You need to understand these models and which services they apply to.

Make sure you understand what AWS charges you for and what is free of charge. For instance, inbound data transfer is free whereas outbound data transfer typically incurs costs.

Some services such as VPC, CloudFormation, and IAM are free but the resources you create with them may not be. You need to understand where costs may be incurred.

AWS accounts can be organized into Organizations for centralized management of policies and consolidated billing. You need to understand the various accounts structures and the benefits and use cases for implementing them.

For instance, you might want separate account structures to manage different policies for production and non-production resources, or you might implement consolidated billing to take advantage of volume discounts.

For billing support, you need to know the services and tools available to you and what levels of support you can get from AWS support plans.

Tools include AWS Cost Explorer, AWS Simple Monthly Calculator, and Total Cost of Ownership (TCO) calculator.

Example questions

Question: *What are two ways an AWS customer can reduce their monthly spend? (choose 2)*

1. Turn off resources that are not being used
2. Use more power efficient instance types
3. Reserve capacity where suitable
4. Be efficient with usage of Security Groups
5. Reduce the amount of data ingress charges

Answer: 1+3, turning off resources that are not used can reduce spend. You can also use reserved instances to reduce the monthly spend at the expense of having to lock into a 1 or 3-year contract – good for stable workloads.

Question: *A company would like to maximize* their *potential volume and RI discounts across multiple accounts and also apply service control policies on member accounts. What can they use gain these benefits?*

1. AWS Budgets
2. AWS Cost Explorer
3. AWS IAM
4. AWS Organizations

Answer: 4, AWS Organizations enables you to create groups of AWS accounts and then centrally manage policies across those accounts. AWS Organizations provides consolidated billing in both feature sets, which allows you set up a single payment method in the organization's master account and still receive an invoice for individual activity in each member account. Volume pricing discounts can be applied to resources.

AWS CLOUD COMPUTING CONCEPTS

Cloud computing is the on-demand delivery of compute power, database storage, applications, and other IT resources through a cloud services platform via the Internet with pay-as-you-go pricing.

Cloud computing provides a simple way to access servers, storage, databases, and a broad set of application services over the Internet.

The following introductory-level article covers some key **AWS concepts** that relate to cloud computing:

- What is Cloud Computing? Cloud vs Legacy IT

The following articles provide some additional information around basic computing concepts:

- Cloud Computing Basics – Compute
- Cloud Computing Basics – Storage
- Cloud Computing Basics – Network
- Cloud Computing Basics – Serverless

A cloud services platform such as Amazon Web Services owns and maintains the network-connected hardware required for these application services, while you provision and use what you need via a web application.

THE 6 ADVANTAGES OF CLOUD

You must understand the following 6 advantages of cloud:

1. Trade capital expense for variable expense.
2. Benefit from massive economies of scale.
3. Stop guessing about capacity.
4. Increase speed and agility.
5. Stop spending money running and maintaining data centers.
6. Go global in minutes.

TRADE CAPITAL EXPENSE FOR VARIABLE EXPENSE

Instead of having to invest heavily in data centers and servers before you know how you're going to use them, you can pay only when you consume computing resources, and pay only for how much you consume.

BENEFIT FROM MASSIVE ECONOMIES OF SCALE

By using cloud computing, you can achieve a lower variable cost than you can get on your own. Because usage from hundreds of thousands of customers is aggregated in the cloud, providers such as AWS can achieve higher economies of scale, which translates into lower pay as-you-go price.

STOP GUESSING ABOUT CAPACITY

Eliminate guessing on your infrastructure capacity needs. When you make a capacity decision prior to deploying an application, you often end up either sitting on expensive idle resources or dealing with limited capacity.

With cloud computing, these problems go away. You can access as much or as little capacity as you need and scale up and down as required with only a few minutes' notice.

INCREASE SPEED AND AGILITY

In a cloud computing environment, new IT resources are only a click away, which means that you reduce the time to make those resources available to your developers from weeks to just minutes.

This results in a dramatic increase in agility for the organization since the cost and time it takes to experiment and develop is significantly lower.

STOP SPENDING MONEY RUNNING AND MAINTAINING DATA CENTERS

Focus on projects that differentiate your business, not the infrastructure. Cloud computing lets you focus on your own customers, rather than on the heavy lifting of racking, stacking, and powering servers.

GO GLOBAL IN MINUTES

Easily deploy your application in multiple regions around the world with just a few clicks. This means you can provide lower latency and a better experience for your customers at minimal cost.

CLOUD COMPUTING MODELS

There are 3 common types of cloud computing model that come up in the exam:

1. Infrastructure as a service (IaaS).
2. Platform as a service (PaaS).
3. Software as a service (SaaS).

INFRASTRUCTURE AS A SERVICE (IAAS)

Infrastructure as a Service (IaaS) contains the basic building blocks for cloud IT and typically provide access to networking features, computers (virtual or on dedicated hardware), and data storage space.

IaaS provides you with the highest level of flexibility and management control over your IT resources and is very similar to the existing IT resources that many IT departments and developers are familiar with today.

PLATFORM AS A SERVICE (PAAS)

Platform as a Service (PaaS) removes the need for your organization to manage the underlying infrastructure (usually hardware and operating systems) and allows you to focus on the deployment and management of your applications.

This helps you be more efficient as you don't need to worry about resource procurement, capacity planning, software maintenance, patching, or any of the other undifferentiated heavy lifting involved in running your application.

SOFTWARE AS A SERVICE (SAAS)

Software as a Service (SaaS) provides you with a completed product that is run and managed by the service provider. In most cases, people referring to Software as a Service are referring to end-user applications.

With a SaaS offering you do not have to think about how the service is maintained or how the underlying infrastructure is managed; you only need to think about how you will use that piece of software.

A common example of a SaaS application is web-based email which you can use to send and receive email without having to manage feature additions to the email product or maintain the servers and operating systems that the email program is running on.

SaaS provides high availability, fault tolerance, scalability an elasticity.

The following article provides some additional information:

- Cloud Computing Service Models – IaaS, PaaS, SaaS

TYPES OF CLOUD DEPLOYMENT

There are 3 common types of cloud deployment that come up in the exam:

1. Public Cloud – e.g. AWS, Microsoft Azure, Google Cloud Platform (GCP).
2. Hybrid Cloud – a mixture of public and private clouds.
3. Private Cloud (on-premises) – a cloud managed in your own data center, e.g. Hyper-V, OpenStack, VMware.

PUBLIC CLOUD

A cloud-based application is fully deployed in the cloud and all parts of the application run in the cloud. Applications in the cloud have either been created in the cloud or have been migrated from an existing infrastructure to take advantage of the benefits of cloud computing.

Cloud-based applications can be built on low-level infrastructure pieces or can use higher level services that provide abstraction from the management, architecting, and scaling requirements of core infrastructure.

HYBRID

A hybrid deployment is a way to connect infrastructure and applications between cloud-based resources and existing resources that are not located in the cloud.

The most common method of hybrid deployment is between the cloud and existing on-premises infrastructure to extend, and grow, an organization's infrastructure into the cloud while connecting cloud resources to the internal system.

ON-PREMISES

The deployment of resources on-premises, using virtualization and resource management tools, is sometimes called the "private cloud."

On-premises deployment doesn't provide many of the benefits of cloud computing but is sometimes sought for its ability to provide dedicated resources.

In most cases this deployment model is the same as legacy IT infrastructure while using application management and virtualization technologies to try and increase resource utilization.

The following article provides some additional information:

- Cloud Computing Deployment Models – Public, Private & Hybrid

CLOUD COMPUTING CONCEPTS

Answers and explanations are provided below after the last question in this section.

Question 1: What is a key cost advantage of moving to the AWS Cloud?

1. Many services are free
2. You can provision what you need and scale on demand
3. You can deploy services using an API
4. You can scale almost limitlessly

Question 2: Which of the following is an advantage of cloud computing?

1. Trade capital expense for variable expense
2. Trade operational expense for capital expense
3. Go global in days
4. Outsource all application development

CLOUD COMPUTING CONCEPTS ANSWERS

Question 1: What is a key cost advantage of moving to the AWS Cloud?

1. Many services are free
2. You can provision what you need and scale on demand
3. You can deploy services using an API
4. You can scale almost limitlessly

Answer: 2

Explanation:

1 is incorrect. This is true, but it's not the best reason to move to AWS as you still have to pay for most compute and storage services

2 is correct. This is a great reason to move to the cloud and a key cost benefit. This means you are only ever paying for resources that you are actually using, with little or no idle capacity

3 is incorrect. This is an advantage of the cloud, but not related to cost

4 is incorrect. This is true but not a key cost advantage

Question 2: Which of the following is an advantage of cloud computing?

1. Trade capital expense for variable expense
2. Trade operational expense for capital expense
3. Go global in days
4. Outsource all application development

Answer: 1

Explanation:

1 is correct. This is an advantage of cloud computing. You can reduce or eliminate capital expense in favor of variable operational expenses

2 is incorrect. This is the opposite of what you want, it is better to trade capital expense for operational/variable expense

3 is incorrect. It should be "Go global in minutes"!

4 is incorrect. You cannot outsource all application development with AWS

AWS GLOBAL INFRASTRUCTURE

This article covers AWS Global Infrastructure training which is a key technology area covered in the Cloud Practitioner exam blueprint. The AWS infrastructure is built around Regions and Availability Zones (AZs).

An AWS Region is a physical location in the world where AWS have multiple AZs.

AZs consist of one or more discrete data centers, each with redundant power, networking, and connectivity, housed in separate facilities.

Each region is completely independent. Each Availability Zone is isolated, but the Availability Zones in a region are connected through low-latency links.

AWS are constantly expanding around the world and currently there are:

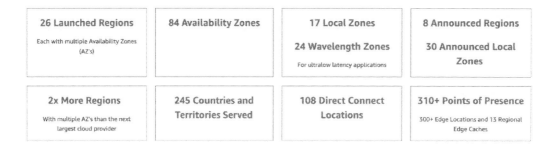

REGIONS

A region is a geographical area.

Each region consists of 2 or more availability zones.

Each Amazon Region is designed to be completely isolated from the other Amazon Regions.

Each AWS Region has multiple Availability Zones and data centers.

You can replicate data within a region and between regions using private or public Internet connections.

You retain complete control and ownership over the region in which your data is physically located, making it easy to meet regional compliance and data residency requirements.

Note that there is a charge for data transfer between regions.

When you launch an EC2 instance, you must select an AMI that's in the same region. If the AMI is in another region, you can copy the AMI to the region you're using.

Regions and Endpoints:
- When you work with an instance using the command line interface or API actions, you must specify its regional endpoint.
- To reduce data latency in your applications, most Amazon Web Services offer a regional endpoint to make your requests.
- An endpoint is a URL that is the entry point for a web service.

- For example, https://dynamodb.us-west-2.amazonaws.com is an entry point for the Amazon DynamoDB service.

AVAILABILITY ZONES

Availability Zones are physically separate and isolated from each other.

AZs span one or more data centers and have direct, low-latency, high throughput, and redundant network connections between each other.

Each AZ is designed as an independent failure zone.

When you launch an instance, you can select an Availability Zone or let AWS choose one for you.

If you distribute your EC2 instances across multiple Availability Zones and one instance fails, you can design your application so that an instance in another Availability Zone can handle requests.

You can also use Elastic IP addresses to mask the failure of an instance in one Availability Zone by rapidly remapping the address to an instance in another Availability Zone.

An Availability Zone is represented by a region code followed by a letter identifier; for example, *us-east-1a.*

To ensure that resources are distributed across the Availability Zones for a region, AWS independently map Availability Zones to names for each AWS account.

For example, the Availability Zone *us-east-1a* for your AWS account might not be the same location as us-east-1a for another AWS account.

To coordinate Availability Zones across accounts, you must use the *AZ ID*, which is a unique and consistent identifier for an Availability Zone.

AZs are physically separated within a typical metropolitan region and are in lower risk flood plains.

AZs use discrete UPS and onsite backup generation facilities and are fed via different grids from independent facilities.

AZs are all redundantly connected to multiple tier-1 transit providers.

The following graphic shows three AWS Regions each of which has three Availability Zones:

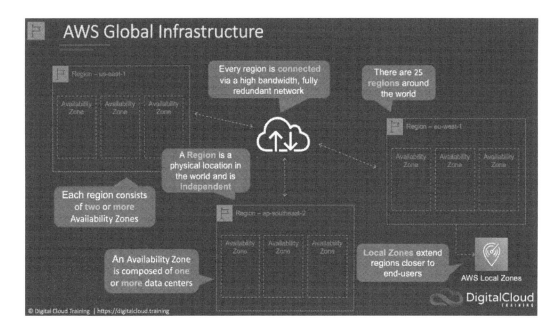

LOCAL ZONES

AWS Local Zones place compute, storage, database, and other select AWS services closer to end-users.

With AWS Local Zones, you can easily run highly demanding applications that require single-digit millisecond latencies to your end-users.

Each AWS Local Zone location is an extension of an AWS Region where you can run your latency sensitive applications using AWS services such as Amazon Elastic Compute Cloud, Amazon Virtual Private Cloud, Amazon Elastic Block Store, Amazon File Storage, and Amazon Elastic Load Balancing in geographic proximity to end-users.

AWS Local Zones provide a high-bandwidth, secure connection between local workloads and those running in the AWS Region, allowing you to seamlessly connect to the full range of in-region services through the same APIs and tool sets.

AWS WAVELENGTH

AWS Wavelength enables developers to build applications that deliver single-digit millisecond latencies to mobile devices and end-users.

AWS developers can deploy their applications to Wavelength Zones, AWS infrastructure deployments that embed AWS compute and storage services within the telecommunications providers' datacenters at the edge of the 5G networks, and seamlessly access the breadth of AWS services in the region.

AWS Wavelength brings AWS services to the edge of the 5G network, minimizing the latency to connect to an application from a mobile device.

AWS OUTPOSTS

AWS Outposts bring native AWS services, infrastructure, and operating models to virtually any data center, co-location space, or on-premises facility.

You can use the same AWS APIs, tools, and infrastructure across on-premises and the AWS cloud to deliver a truly consistent hybrid experience.

AWS Outposts is designed for connected environments and can be used to support workloads that need to remain on-premises due to low latency or local data processing needs.

EDGE LOCATIONS AND REGIONAL EDGE CACHES

Edge locations are Content Delivery Network (CDN) endpoints for CloudFront.

There are many more edge locations than regions.

Currently there are over 200 edge locations.

Regional Edge Caches sit between your CloudFront Origin servers and the Edge Locations.

A Regional Edge Cache has a larger cache-width than each of the individual Edge Locations.

The following diagram shows CloudFront Edge locations:

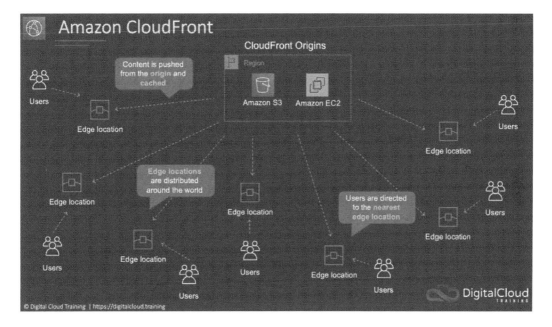

AWS GLOBAL INFRASTRUCTURE QUIZ QUESTIONS

Answers and explanations are provided below after the last question in this section.

Question 1: What is an availability zone composed of?

1. A collection of edge locations
2. A collection of VPCs
3. One or more DCs in a location
4. One or more regions

Question 2: What is an AWS Region composed of?

1. Two or more Virtual Private Clouds (VPC)
2. Two or more availability zones
3. At least one availability zone
4. A collection of EC2 instances

AWS GLOBAL INFRASTRUCTURE ANSWERS

Question 1: What is an availability zone composed of?

1. A collection of edge locations
2. A collection of VPCs
3. One or more DCs in a location
4. One or more regions

Answer: 3

Explanation:

1 is incorrect. An availability zone is not a collection of edge locations.

2 is incorrect. An availability zone is not a collection of VPCs.

3 is correct. Availability Zones are physically separate and isolated from each other. They are located in one or more data centers in a geographical area.

4 is incorrect. Availability zones are contained within regions, not the other way around.

Question 2: What is an AWS Region composed of?

1. Two or more Virtual Private Clouds (VPC)
2. Two or more availability zones
3. At least one availability zone
4. A collection of EC2 instances

Answer: 2

Explanation:

1 is incorrect. Virtual Private Clouds (VPCs), which will be discussed later in the course, are contained within a region but it's not necessary to have more than one VPC in a region

2 is correct. Every region has at least 2 availability zones which are composed of one or more data centers

3 is incorrect. There are always at least 2 availability zones in a region

4 is incorrect. EC2 instances, which are computer instances, run in a VPC and within a region, but this is not how we define a region

AWS IAM

AWS Identity and Access Management (IAM) is a web service that helps you securely control access to AWS resources.

You use IAM to control who is authenticated (signed in) and authorized (has permissions) to use resources.

IAM makes it easy to provide multiple users secure access to AWS resources.

When you first create an AWS account, you begin with a single sign-in identity that has complete access to all AWS services and resources in the account.

This identity is called the AWS account *root user* and is accessed by signing in with the email address and password that you used to create the account.

IAM can be used to manage:

- Users.
- Groups.
- Access policies.
- Roles.
- User credentials.
- User password policies.
- Multi-factor authentication (MFA).
- API keys for programmatic access (CLI).

IAM provides the following features:

- Shared access to your AWS account.
- Granular permissions.
- Secure access to AWS resources for application that run on Amazon EC2.
- Multi-Factor authentication.
- Identity federation.
- Identity information for assurance.
- PCI DSS compliance.
- Integrated with many AWS services.
- Eventually consistent.
- Free to use.

You can work with AWS Identity and Access Management in any of the following ways:

- AWS Management Console.
- AWS Command Line Tools.
- AWS SDKs.
- IAM HTTPS API.

By default, new users are created with NO access to any AWS services – they can only login to the AWS console.

Permission must be explicitly granted to allow a user to access an AWS service.

IAM users are individuals who have been granted access to an AWS account.

Each IAM user has three main components:

- A username.
- A password.
- Permissions to access various resources.

You can apply granular permissions with IAM.

You can assign users individual security credentials such as access keys, passwords, and multi-factor authentication devices.

IAM is not used for application-level authentication.

Identity Federation (including AD, Facebook etc.) can be configured allowing secure access to resources in an AWS account without creating an IAM user account.

Multi-factor authentication (MFA) can be enabled/enforced for the AWS account and for individual users under the account.

MFA uses an authentication device that continually generates random, six-digit, single-use authentication codes.

You can authenticate using an MFA device in the following two ways:

- Through the **AWS Management Console** – the user is prompted for a user name, password, and authentication code.
- Using the **AWS API** – restrictions are added to IAM policies and developers can request temporary security credentials and pass MFA parameters in their AWS STS API requests.
- Using the **AWS CLI** by obtaining temporary security credentials from STS (aws sts get-session-token).

It is a best practice to always setup multi-factor authentication on the root account.

IAM is universal (global) and does not apply to regions.

IAM replicates data across multiple data centers around the world.

The "root account" is the account created when you setup the AWS account. It has complete Admin access and is the only account that has this access by default.

It is a best practice to avoid using the root account for anything other than billing.

Power user access allows all permissions except the management of groups and users in IAM.

Temporary security credentials consist of the AWS access key ID, secret access key, and security token.

IAM can assign temporary security credentials to provide users with temporary access to services/resources.

To sign-in you must provide your account ID or account alias in addition to a user name and password.

The sign-in URL includes the account ID or account alias, e.g.:

https://***My_AWS_Account_ID***.signin.aws.amazon.com/console/.

Alternatively, you can sign-in at the following URL and enter your account ID or alias manually:

https://console.aws.amazon.com/

IAM integrates with many different AWS services.

Authentication Methods

Console password:

- A password that the user can enter to sign in to interactive sessions such as the AWS Management Console.
- You can allow users to change their own passwords.
- You can allow selected IAM users to change their passwords by disabling the option for all users and using an IAM policy to grant permissions for the selected users.

Access Keys:

- A combination of an access key ID and a secret access key.
- You can assign two active access keys to a user at a time.
- These can be used to make programmatic calls to AWS when using the **API** in program code or at a command prompt when using the **AWS CLI** or the **AWS PowerShell** tools.
- You can create, modify, view, or rotate access keys.
- When created IAM returns the access key ID and secret access key.
- The secret access is returned only at creation time and if lost a new key must be created.
- Ensure access keys and secret access keys are stored securely.
- Users can be given access to change their own keys through IAM policy (not from the console).
- You can disable a user's access key which prevents it from being used for API calls.

Server certificates:

- SSL/TLS certificates that you can use to authenticate with some AWS services.
- AWS recommends that you use the AWS Certificate Manager (ACM) to provision, manage and deploy your server certificates.
- Use IAM only when you must support HTTPS connections in a region that is not supported by ACM.

IAM USERS

An IAM user is an entity that represents a person or service.

Can be assigned:

- An access key ID and secret access key for programmatic access to the AWS API, CLI, SDK, and other development tools.
- A password for access to the management console.

By default, users cannot access anything in your account.

The account root user credentials are the email address used to create the account and a password.

The root account has full administrative permissions, and these cannot be restricted.

Best practice for root accounts:

- Don't use the root user credentials.
- Don't share the root user credentials.
- Create an IAM user and assign administrative permissions as required.
- Enable MFA.

IAM users can be created to represent applications, and these are known as "service accounts".

You can have up to 5000 users per AWS account.

Each user account has a friendly name and an ARN which uniquely identifies the user across AWS.

A unique ID is also created which is returned only when you create the user using the API, Tools for Windows PowerShell, or the AWS CLI.

You should create individual IAM accounts for users (best practice not to share accounts).

The Access Key ID and Secret Access Key are not the same as a password and cannot be used to login to the AWS console.

The Access Key ID and Secret Access Key can only be used once and must be regenerated if lost.

A password policy can be defined for enforcing password length, complexity etc. (applies to all users).

You can allow or disallow the ability to change passwords using an IAM policy.

Access keys and passwords should be changed regularly.

GROUPS

Groups are collections of users and have policies attached to them.

A group is not an identity and cannot be identified as a principal in an IAM policy.

Use groups to assign permissions to users.

Use the principle of least privilege when assigning permissions.

You cannot nest groups (groups within groups).

ROLES

Roles are created and then "assumed" by trusted entities and define a set of permissions for making AWS service requests.

With IAM Roles you can delegate permissions to resources for users and services without using permanent credentials (e.g. user name and password).

IAM users or AWS services can assume a role to obtain temporary security credentials that can be used to make AWS API calls.

You can delegate using roles.

There are no credentials associated with a role (password or access keys).

IAM users can temporarily assume a role to take on permissions for a specific task.

A role can be assigned to a federated user who signs in using an external identity provider.

Temporary credentials are primarily used with IAM roles and automatically expire.

Roles can be assumed temporarily through the console or programmatically with the **AWS CLI**, **Tools for Windows PowerShell,** or the **API.**

IAM roles with EC2 instances:

- IAM roles can be used for granting applications running on EC2 instances permissions to AWS API requests using instance profiles.
- Only one role can be assigned to an EC2 instance at a time.
- A role can be assigned at the EC2 instance creation time or at any time afterwards.
- When using the AWS CLI or API instance profiles must be created manually (it's automatic and transparent through the console).
- Applications retrieve temporary security credentials from the instance metadata.

Role Delegation:

- Create an IAM role with two policies:
  - Permissions policy – grants the user of the role the required permissions on a resource.
  - Trust policy – specifies the trusted accounts that are allowed to assume the role.
- Wildcards (*) cannot be specified as a principal.
- A permissions policy must also be attached to the user in the trusted account.

POLICIES

Policies are documents that define permissions and can be applied to users, groups, and roles.

Policy documents are written in JSON (key value pair that consists of an attribute and a value).

All permissions are implicitly denied by default.

The most restrictive policy is applied.

The IAM policy simulator is a tool to help you understand, test, and validate the effects of access control policies.

The Condition element can be used to apply further conditional logic.

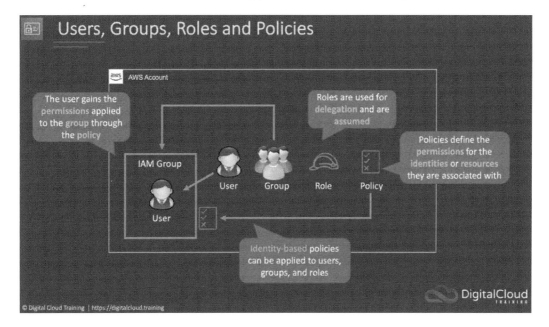

AWS SECURITY TOKEN SERVICE (AWS STS)

The AWS STS is a web service that enables you to request temporary, limited-privilege credentials for IAM users or for users that you authenticate (federated users).

Temporary security credentials work almost identically to long-term access key credentials that IAM users can use, with the following differences:

- Temporary security credentials are short-term.
- They can be configured to last anywhere from a few minutes to several hours.
- After the credentials expire, AWS no longer recognizes them or allows any kind of access to API requests made with them.
- Temporary security credentials are not stored with the user but are generated dynamically and provided to the user when requested.
- When (or even before) the temporary security credentials expire, the user can request new credentials, if the user requesting them still has permission to do so.

Advantages of STS are:

- You do not have to distribute or embed long-term AWS security credentials with an application.
- You can provide access to your AWS resources to users without having to define an AWS identity for them (temporary security credentials are the basis for IAM Roles and ID Federation).
- The temporary security credentials have a limited lifetime, so you do not have to rotate them or explicitly revoke them when they're no longer needed.
- After temporary security credentials expire, they cannot be reused (you can specify how long the credentials are valid for, up to a maximum limit)

Users can come from three sources.

1) **Federation (typically AD):**
   - Uses SAML 2.0.
   - Grants temporary access based on the users AD credentials.
   - Does not need to be a user in IAM.
   - Single sign-on allows users to login to the AWS console without assigning IAM credentials.

2) **Federation with Mobile Apps:**
   - Use Facebook/Amazon/Google or other OpenID providers to login.

3) **Cross Account Access:**
   - Allows users from one AWS account access resources in another.
   - To make a request in a different account the resource in that account must have an attached resource-based policy with the permissions you need.
   - Or you must assume a role (identity-based policy) within that account with the permissions you need.

IAM BEST PRACTICES

Lock away the AWS root user access keys.

Create individual IAM users.

Use AWS defined policies to assign permissions whenever possible.

Use groups to assign permissions to IAM users.

Grant least privilege.

Use access levels to review IAM permissions.

Configure a strong password policy for users.

Enable MFA.

Use roles for applications that run on AWS EC2 instances.

Delegate by using roles instead of sharing credentials.

Rotate credentials regularly.

Remove unnecessary credentials.

Use policy conditions for extra security.

Monitor activity in your AWS account.

AWS IDENTITY AND ACCESS MANAGEMENT QUIZ QUESTIONS

Answers and explanations are provided below after the last question in this section.

Question 1: An access key ID and secret access key is associated with which IAM entity?

1. User
2. Group
3. Role
4. Policy

Question 2: What is the main credential for an AWS root account?

1. Administrator
2. root
3. The email address used to create the account
4. The account number

Question 3: Which principle should be used when assigning permissions to users or groups?

1. Most privilege
2. Least privilege
3. Nesting
4. Most restrictive

Question 4: Which IAM entity can be used to delegate permissions?

1. User
2. Group
3. Role
4. Policy

Question 5: How can you add an extra level of security to your root account?

1. By adding an access key ID and secret access key
2. By adding multi-factor authentication (MFA)
3. By setting a strong password
4. By deleting the root account

Question 6: Which of the following is NOT an IAM security best practice?

1. Use groups to assign permissions to IAM users
2. Configure a strong password policy for users
3. Grant most privilege
4. Rotate credentials regularly

Question 7: By default, users are created with what permissions?

1. Full permissions
2. No permissions
3. Minimal permissions
4. No access to the AWS management console

AWS IDENTITY AND ACCESS MANAGEMENT ANSWERS

Question 1: An access key ID and secret access key is associated with which IAM entity?

1. User
2. Group
3. Role
4. Policy

Answer: 1

Explanation:

1 is correct. An access key ID and secret access key is associated with a user and is used for granting programmatic access using the CLI or API

2 is incorrect. You cannot assign an access key ID and secret access key to a group

3 is incorrect. You cannot assign an access key ID and secret access key to a role

4 is incorrect. You cannot assign an access key ID and secret access key to a policy

Question 2: What is the main credential for an AWS root account?

1. Administrator
2. root
3. The email address used to create the account
4. The account number

Answer: 3

Explanation:

1 is incorrect. Administrator is not a credential used with AWS

2 is incorrect. root is the username associated with some operating systems such as Linux, it is not an actual user name used in your AWS account

3 is correct. The account root user credential is the email address used to create the account and a password

4 is incorrect. The account number or alias is used to sign in when using an IAM account, rather than the root credentials

Question 3: Which principle should be used when assigning permissions to users or groups?

1. Most privilege
2. Least privilege
3. Nesting
4. Most restrictive

Answer: 2

Explanation:

> **1 is incorrect.** This would be a bad practice as it would provide more privileges to users than they need to perform their jobs

> **2 is correct.** When assigning permissions always grant the least privileges required. This is a security best practice

> **3 is incorrect.** Nesting is not a security practice

> **4 is incorrect.** This would lead to users having too few permissions. You always want to make sure people can perform their jobs whilst not providing too much freedom.

Question 4: Which IAM entity can be used to delegate permissions?

1. User
2. Group
3. Role
4. Policy

Answer: 3

Explanation:

> **1 is incorrect.** You cannot delegate using users

> **2 is incorrect.** You cannot delegate using Groups, but you can assign permissions to multiple users through groups.

> **3 is correct.** You can delegate permissions using roles. It's a great way to provide permissions to resources for users and services without using permanent credentials

> **4 is incorrect.** You cannot delegate using a policy. You delegate using a role and you define permissions to the role through a policy

Question 5: How can you add an extra level of security to your root account?

1. By adding an access key ID and secret access key
2. By adding multi-factor authentication (MFA)
3. By setting a strong password
4. By deleting the root account

Answer: 2

Explanation:

> **1 is incorrect.** No, this will not add security. In fact, it's a security best practice to either remove these from your root account or at least minimize their usage

> **2 is correct.** Adding multi-factor authentication (MFA) to your root account adds an extra level of security as a device is needed to login as well as a username and password. This is a security best practice

> **3 is incorrect.** This is definitely recommended, however this isn't considered an extra level of security

> **4 is incorrect.** You cannot delete the root account

Question 6: Which of the following is NOT an IAM security best practice?

1. Use groups to assign permissions to IAM users
2. Configure a strong password policy for users
3. Grant most privilege
4. Rotate credentials regularly

Answer: 3

Explanation:

1 is incorrect. This is an IAM security best practice

2 is incorrect. This is an IAM security best practice

3 is correct. This is not a security best practice. AWS recommend granting least privilege when assigning permissions

4 is incorrect. This is an IAM security best practice

Question 7: By default, users are created with what permissions?

1. Full permissions
2. No permissions
3. Minimal permissions
4. No access to the AWS management console

Answer: 2

Explanation:

1 is incorrect. Users are not created with full permissions

2 is correct. Users are created with no permissions. You can then assign permissions using groups and policies

3 is incorrect. Users are not created with minimal permissions, they are created with no permissions

4 is incorrect. Users will have access to the AWS management console; however they won't have any permissions to services by default

AWS COMPUTE

This article discusses AWS Compute in the context of the AWS Certified Cloud Practitioner Exam. This is one of the key technology areas covered in the exam guide.

AMAZON EC2

Amazon Elastic Compute Cloud (Amazon EC2) is a web service with which you can run virtual server "instances" in the cloud.

Amazon EC2 instances can run the Windows, Linux, or MacOS operating systems.

The EC2 simple web service interface allows you to obtain and configure capacity with minimal friction.

EC2 is designed to make web-scale cloud computing easier for developers.

Amazon EC2 changes the economics of computing by allowing you to pay only for capacity that you use.

Amazon EC2 provides developers the tools to build failure resilient applications and isolate them from common failure scenarios.

Benefits of EC2 include:

- **Elastic Web-Scale computing** – you can increase or decrease capacity within minutes not hours and commission one to thousands of instances simultaneously.
- **Completely controlled** – You have complete control include root access to each instance and can stop and start instances without losing data and using web service APIs.
- **Flexible Cloud Hosting Services** – you can choose from multiple instance types, operating systems, and software packages as well as instances with varying memory, CPU, and storage configurations.
- **Integrated** – EC2 is integrated with most AWS services such as S3, RDS, and VPC to provide a complete, secure solution.
- **Reliable** – EC2 offers a highly reliable environment where replacement instances can be rapidly and predictably commissioned with SLAs of 99.99% for each region.
- **Secure** – EC2 works in conjunction with VPC to provide a secure location with an IP address range you specify and offers Security Groups, Network ACLs, and IPSec VPN features.
- **Inexpensive** – Amazon passes on the financial benefits of scale by charging very low rates and on a capacity consumed basis.

An Amazon Machine Image (AMI) is a special type of virtual appliance that is used to create a virtual machine within the Amazon Elastic Compute Cloud ("EC2").

An AMI includes the following:

- One or more **EBS** snapshots, or, for instance-store-backed AMIs, a template for the root volume of the instance (for example, an operating system, an application server, and applications).
- Launch permissions that control which AWS accounts can use the AMI to launch

instances.

- A block device mapping that specifies the volumes to attach to the instance when it's launched.

AMIs come in three main categories:

- **Community AMIs** – free to use, generally you just select the operating system you want.
- **AWS Marketplace AMIs** – pay to use, generally come packaged with additional, licensed software.
- **My AMIs** – AMIs that you create yourself.

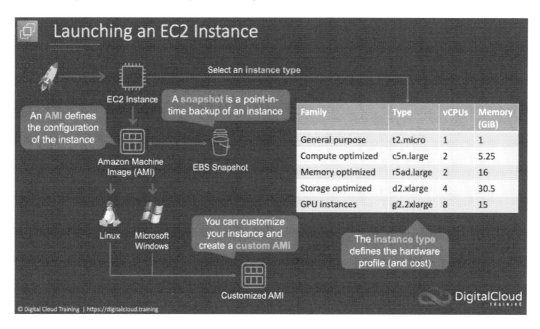

Metadata and User Data:

- User data is data that is supplied by the user at instance launch in the form of a script.
- Instance metadata is data about your instance that you can use to configure or manage the running instance.
- User data is limited to 16KB.
- User data and metadata are not encrypted.
- Instance metadata is available at http://169.254.169.254/latest/meta-data.

The Instance Metadata Query tool allows you to query the instance metadata without having to type out the full URI or category names.

PRICING

On-demand:

- Good for users that want the low cost and flexibility of EC2 without any up-front payment or long-term commitment.
- Applications with short term, spiky, or unpredictable workloads that cannot be

interrupted.
- Applications being developed or tested on EC2 for the first time.

Reserved:

- Applications with steady state or predictable usage.
- Applications that require reserved capacity.
- Users can make up-front payments to reduce their total computing costs even further.
- Standard Reserved Instances (RIs) provide up to 75% off on-demand price.
- Convertible RIs provide up to 54% off on-demand price – provides the capability to change the attributes of the RI if the exchange results in the creation of RIs of equal or greater value.
- Scheduled RIs are available to launch within the time window you reserve. This option allows you to match your capacity reservation to a predictable recurring schedule that only requires a fraction of a day, a week, or a month.

Spot:

- Applications that have flexible start and end times.
- Applications that are only feasible at very low compute prices.
- Users with an urgent need for a large amount of additional compute capacity.
- If Amazon terminate your instances, you do not pay, if you terminate you pay for the hour.

Dedicated hosts:

- Physical servers dedicated just for your use.
- You then have control over which instances are deployed on that host.
- Available as On-Demand or with Dedicated Host Reservation.
- Useful if you have server-bound software licenses that use metrics like per-core, per-socket, or per-VM.
- Each dedicated host can only run one EC2 instance size and type.
- Good for regulatory compliance or licensing requirements.
- Predictable performance.
- Complete isolation.
- Most expensive option.
- Billing is per host.

Dedicated instances:

- Virtualized instances on hardware just for you.
- Also uses physically dedicated EC2 servers.
- Does not provide the additional visibility and controls of dedicated hosts (e.g. how instances are placed on a server).
- Billing is per instance.
- May share hardware with other non-dedicated instances in the same account.
- Available as On-Demand, Reserved Instances, and Spot Instances.
- Cost additional $2 per hour per region.

Savings Plans:

- Savings Plans is a flexible pricing model that provides savings of up to 72% on your AWS compute usage.
- This pricing model offers lower prices on Amazon EC2 instances usage, regardless of instance family, size, OS, tenancy, or AWS Region.
- Also applies to AWS Fargate and AWS Lambda usage.

INSTANCE TYPES

Amazon EC2 provides a wide selection of instance types optimized to fit different use cases.

Instance types comprise varying combinations of CPU, memory, storage, and networking capacity and give you the flexibility to choose the appropriate mix of resources for your applications.

Each instance type includes one or more instance sizes, allowing you to scale your resources to the requirements of your target workload.

The table below helps you to understand some of the various EC2 instance families and their intended use case:

Family	Hint	Purpose/Design
D	DATA	Heavy data usage (e.g. file servers, DWs)
R	RAM	Memory optimized
M	MAIN	General purpose (e.g. app servers)
C	COMPUTE	Compute optimized
G	GRAPHICS	Graphics intensive workloads
I	IOPS	Storage I/O optimized (e.g. NoSQL, DWs)
F	FAST	FPGA hardware acceleration for applications
T	CHEAP (think T2)	Lowest cost (e.g. T2-micro)
P	GPU	GPU requirements
X	EXTREME RAM	Heavy memory usage (e.g. SAP HANA, Apache Spark)
U	HIGH MEMORY	High memory and bare metal performance – use for in memory DBs including SAP HANA
Z	HGH COMPUTE & MEMORY	Fast CPU, high memory, and NVMe-based SSDs – use when high overall performance is required
H	HIGH DISK THROUGHPUT	Up to 16 TB of HDD-based local storage

AMAZON ELASTIC CONTAINER SERVICE (ECS)

Amazon Elastic Container Service (ECS) is another product in the AWS Compute category. It provides a highly scalable, high performance container management service that supports Docker containers and allows you to easily run applications on a managed cluster of Amazon EC2 instances.

Amazon ECS eliminates the need for you to install, operate, and scale your own cluster management infrastructure.

Using API calls you can launch and stop container-enabled applications, query the complete state of clusters, and access many familiar features like security groups, Elastic Load Balancing, EBS volumes and IAM roles.

Amazon ECS can be used to schedule the placement of containers across clusters based on resource needs and availability requirements.

An Amazon ECS launch type determines the type of infrastructure on which your tasks and services are hosted.

There are two launch types, and the table below describes some of the differences between the two launch types:

Amazon EC2	Amazon Fargate
You explicitly provision EC2 instances	The control plane asks for resources and Fargate automatically provisions
You're responsible for upgrading, patching, care of EC2 pool	Fargate provisions compute as needed
You must handle cluster optimization	Fargate handles cluster optimization
More granular control over infrastructure	Limited control, as infrastructure is automated

The Elastic container registry (ECR) is a managed AWS Docker registry service for storing, managing, and deploying Docker images.

There is no additional charge for Amazon ECS. You pay for AWS resources (e.g. EC2 instances or EBS volumes) you create to store and run your application.

Amazon ECR is integrated with Amazon EC2 Container Service (ECS).

With Amazon ECR, there are no upfront fees or commitments. You pay only for the amount of data you store in your repositories and data transferred to the Internet.

AWS LAMBDA

AWS Lambda is a serverless computing technology that allows you to run code without provisioning or managing servers.

AWS Lambda executes code only when needed and scales automatically.

You pay only for the compute time you consume (you pay nothing when your code is not running).

Benefits of AWS Lambda:

- No servers to manage.
- Continuous scaling.
- Millisecond billing.
- Integrates with almost all other AWS services.

Primary use cases for AWS Lambda:

- Data processing.
- Real-time file processing.
- Real-time stream processing.
- Build serverless backends for web, mobile, IOT, and 3rd party API requests.

AMAZON LIGHTSAIL

Amazon LightSail Instances

Amazon LightSail is one of the newest services in the AWS Compute suite of products. Amazon LightSail is great for users who do not have deep AWS technical expertise as it makes it very easy to provision compute services.

Amazon LightSail provides developers compute, storage, and networking capacity and capabilities to deploy and manage websites, web applications, and databases in the cloud.

Amazon LightSail includes everything you need to launch your project quickly – a virtual machine, SSD-based storage, data transfer, DNS management, and a static IP.

Amazon LightSail provides preconfigured virtual private servers (instances) that include everything required to deploy and application or create a database.

The underlying infrastructure and operating system are managed by Amazon LightSail.

Best suited to projects that require a few dozen instances or fewer.

Provides a simple management interface.

Good for blogs, websites, web applications, e-commerce etc.

Can deploy load balancers and attach block storage.

Public API.

Limited to 20 Amazon LightSail instances, 5 static IPs, 3 DNS zones, 20 TB block storage, 40 databases, and 5 load balancers per account.

Up to 20 certificates per calendar year.

Can connect to each other and other AWS resources through public Internet and private (VPC peering) networking.

Application templates include WordPress, WordPress Multisite, Drupal, Joomla!, Magento, Redmine, LAMP, Nginx (LEMP), MEAN, Node.js, and more.

Amazon LightSail currently supports 6 Linux or Unix-like distributions: Amazon Linux, CentOS, Debian, FreeBSD, OpenSUSE, and Ubuntu, as well as 2 Windows Server versions: 2012 R2 and 2016.

AMAZON LIGHTSAIL DATABASES

Amazon LightSail databases are instances that are dedicated to running databases.

An Amazon LightSail database can contain multiple user-created databases, and you can access it by using the same tools and applications that you use with a stand-alone database.

Amazon LightSail managed databases provide an easy, low maintenance way to store your data in the cloud.

Amazon LightSail manages a range of maintenance activities and security for your database and its underlying infrastructure.

Amazon LightSail automatically backs up your database and allows point in time restore from the past 7 days using the database restore tool.

Amazon LightSail databases support the latest major versions of MySQL. Currently, these versions are 5.6, 5.7, and 8.0 for MySQL.

Amazon LightSail databases are available in Standard and High Availability plans.

High Availability plans add redundancy and durability to your database, by automatically creating standby database in a separate Availability Zone.

Amazon LightSail is very affordable.

Amazon LightSail plans are billed on an on-demand hourly rate, so you pay only for what you use.

For every Amazon LightSail plan you use, we charge you the fixed hourly price, up to the maximum monthly plan cost.

AWS ELASTIC BEANSTALK

AWS Elastic Beanstalk is the fastest and simplest way to get web applications up and running on AWS.

Developers simply upload their application code, and the service automatically handles all the details such as resource provisioning, load balancing, auto-scaling, and monitoring.

Elastic Beanstalk is ideal if you have a PHP, Java, Python, Ruby, Node.js, .NET, Go, or Docker web application.

Elastic Beanstalk uses core AWS services such as Amazon EC2, Amazon Elastic Container Service (Amazon ECS), Auto Scaling, and Elastic Load Balancing to easily support applications that need to scale to serve millions of users.

AWS BATCH

AWS Batch enables developers, scientists, and engineers to run hundreds of thousands of batch computing jobs easily and efficiently on AWS.

AWS Batch dynamically provisions the optimal quantity and type of compute resources (e.g., CPU or memory optimized instances) based on the volume and specific resource requirements of the batch jobs submitted.

With AWS Batch, you simply package the code for your batch jobs, specify their dependencies, and submit your batch job using the AWS Management Console, CLIs, or SDKs.

AWS Batch allows you to specify execution parameters and job dependencies and facilitates integration with a broad range of popular batch computing workflow engines and languages (e.g., Pegasus WMS, Luigi, and AWS Step Functions).

AWS Batch efficiently and dynamically provisions and scales Amazon EC2 and Spot Instances based on the requirements of your jobs. AWS Batch provides default job queues and compute environment definitions that enable you to get started quickly.

AWS COMPUTE QUIZ QUESTIONS

Answers and explanations are provided below after the last question in this section.

Question: Question 1: Which of the following is NOT a benefit of AWS Lambda?

1. No servers to manage
2. Pay only when your code is running
3. Continuous scaling
4. Multiple instance types to choose from

Question 2: Which service can assist a developer with quickly deploying and managing a web application on AWS?

1. AWS CloudFormation
2. AWS Elastic Beanstalk

Question 3: AWS Elastic Beanstalk is an example of which cloud computing service model?

1. On-premises
2. Infrastructure as a Service (IaaS)
3. Platform as a Service (PaaS)
4. Software as a Service (SaaS)

Question 4: What is a benefit of Amazon EC2 compared to traditional servers?

1. You can use specialized hardware
2. You have more control over the operating system
3. You can scale elastically within minutes
4. You get more compute power in the cloud

Question 5: How can you run commands on an Amazon EC2 instance at launch time?

1. With metadata
2. With user data
3. With a container
4. With a snapshot

Question 6: Which service allows you to run Docker containers on AWS?

1. Amazon EC2
2. AWS Lambda
3. Amazon ECS
4. Amazon EBS

Question 7: Which service is good for running compute workloads for people who don't have technical expertise with AWS?

1. Amazon ECS
2. Amazon EC2

3. Amazon LightSail
4. AWS Lambda

AWS COMPUTE ANSWERS

Question: Question 1: Which of the following is NOT a benefit of AWS Lambda?

1. No servers to manage
2. Pay only when your code is running
3. Continuous scaling
4. Multiple instance types to choose from

Answer: 4

Explanation:

1 is incorrect. This is a benefit of AWS Lambda - there are no servers to manage which is why it is known as a "serverless" service

2 is incorrect. You do only pay when your code is running, and this is a great benefit of AWS Lambda

3 is incorrect. AWS Lambda includes continuous scaling which means it elastically adjusts to demand

4 is correct. As AWS Lambda is a serverless service, there are no instance types to choose from

Question 2: Which service can assist a developer with quickly deploying and managing a web application on AWS?

1. AWS CloudFormation
2. AWS Elastic Beanstalk

Answer: 2

Explanation:

1 is incorrect. Think of CloudFormation as deploying infrastructure as code, whilst Elastic Beanstalk is more focused on deploying applications on EC2 (PaaS)

2 is correct. AWS Elastic Beanstalk can be used to quickly deploy and manage applications in the AWS Cloud

Question 3: AWS Elastic Beanstalk is an example of which cloud computing service model?

1. On-premises
2. Infrastructure as a Service (IaaS)
3. Platform as a Service (PaaS)
4. Software as a Service (SaaS)

Answer: 3

Explanation:

1 is incorrect. Elastic Beanstalk cannot be used on-premises

2 is incorrect. An example of IaaS is Amazon EC2

3 is correct. Elastic Beanstalk is considered to be a PaaS service. This means the underlying infrastructure and the runtime engine are managed for you and you only need to upload the code

4 is incorrect. Examples of SaaS are Salesforce, Facebook and Gmail

Question 4: What is a benefit of Amazon EC2 compared to traditional servers?

1. You can use specialized hardware
2. You have more control over the operating system
3. You can scale elastically within minutes
4. You get more compute power in the cloud

Answer: 3

Explanation:

1 is incorrect. You cannot use specialized hardware in the cloud. You launch instances on the AWS platform and have no control over the hardware they use

2 is incorrect. You don't have any more control over the operating system in the cloud as in both on-premise and the cloud you have full control

3 is correct. This is a key benefit of the AWS Cloud. You can elastically increase or decrease capacity by changing instance types whenever you need to

4 is incorrect. This is not necessarily true. You can build very powerful compute platforms in your own data center (however it would be very expensive)

Question 5: How can you run commands on an Amazon EC2 instance at launch time?

1. With metadata
2. With user data
3. With a container
4. With a snapshot

Answer: 2

Explanation:

1 is incorrect. Metadata is information about the instance. You can use metadata for finding information such as the availability zone an instance is in or its IP address

2 is correct. User data can be run at instance launch time. You can use it to run commands

3 is incorrect. Containers are another type of compute type; you cannot use a container to run commands on an EC2 instance at launch time

4 is incorrect. Snapshots are copies of EBS volumes that can be used as a backup

Question 6: Which service allows you to run Docker containers on AWS?

1. Amazon EC2
2. AWS Lambda
3. Amazon ECS
4. Amazon EBS

Answer: 3

Explanation:

1 is incorrect. Amazon EC2 is not the service that enables you to use Docker. However, with the EC2 launch type it is used to run the container platform

2 is incorrect. AWS Lambda is used to run functions, not Docker containers

3 is correct. Amazon Elastic Container Service (ECS) is used to run Docker containers on AWS

4 is incorrect. Amazon Elastic Block Store (EBS) is a storage solution that creates "virtual hard drives in the cloud"

Question 7: Which service is good for running compute workloads for people who don't have technical expertise with AWS?

1. Amazon ECS
2. Amazon EC2
3. Amazon LightSail
4. AWS Lambda

Answer: 3

Explanation:

1 is incorrect. Managing Amazon ECS requires good technical knowledge of AWS

2 is incorrect. Managing Amazon EC2 requires good technical knowledge of AWS

3 is correct. Amazon LightSail is great for users who do not have deep AWS technical expertise as it makes it very easy to provision compute services

4 is incorrect. Managing AWS Lambda requires good technical knowledge of AWS

AWS STORAGE

This article discusses AWS Compute in the context of the AWS Certified Cloud Practitioner Exam. This is one of the key technology areas covered in the exam guide.

AMAZON SIMPLE STORAGE SERVICE (S3)

Amazon S3 is object storage built to store and retrieve any amount of data from anywhere – web sites and mobile apps, corporate applications, and data from IoT sensors or devices.

You can store any type of file in S3.

S3 is designed to deliver 99.999999999% durability, and stores data for millions of applications used by market leaders in every industry.

S3 provides comprehensive security and compliance capabilities that meet even the most stringent regulatory requirements.

S3 gives customers flexibility in the way they manage data for cost optimization, access control, and compliance.

Typical use cases include:

- **Backup and Storage** – Provide data backup and storage services for others.
- **Application Hosting** – Provide services that deploy, install, and manage web applications.
- **Media Hosting** – Build a redundant, scalable, and highly available infrastructure that hosts video, photo, or music uploads and downloads.
- **Software Delivery** – Host your software applications that customers can download.
- **Static Website** – you can configure a static website to run from an S3 bucket.

S3 provides query-in-place functionality, allowing you to run powerful analytics directly on your data at rest in S3. And Amazon S3 is the most supported cloud storage service available, with integration from the largest community of third-party solutions, systems integrator partners, and other AWS services.

Files can be anywhere from 0 bytes to 5 TB.

There is unlimited storage available.

Files are stored in buckets.

Buckets are root level folders.

Any subfolder within a bucket is known as a "folder".

S3 is a universal namespace so bucket names must be unique globally.

There are seven S3 storage classes.

- S3 Standard (durable, immediately available, frequently accessed).
- S3 Intelligent-Tiering (automatically moves data to the most cost-effective tier).
- S3 Standard-IA (durable, immediately available, infrequently accessed).
- S3 One Zone-IA (lower cost for infrequently accessed data with less resilience).
- S3 Glacier Instant Retrieval (data that is rarely accessed and requires retrieval in milliseconds).

- S3 Glacier Flexible Retrieval (archived data, retrieval times in minutes or hours).
- S3 Glacier Deep Archive (lowest cost storage class for long term retention).

The table below provides the details of each Amazon S3 storage class:

	S3 Standard	S3 Intelligent Tiering	S3 Standard-IA	S3 One Zone-IA	S3 Glacier Instant Retrieval	S3 Glacier Flexible Retrieval	S3 Glacier Deep Archive
Designed for durability	11 9s	11 9s	11 9s	11 9s	11 9s	11 9s	11 9s
Designed for availability	99.99%	99.9&	99.9%	99.5%	99.9%	99.99%	99.99%
Availability SLA	99.9%	99%	99%	99%	99%	99.99%	99.9%
Availability Zones	≥3	≥3	≥3	1	≥3	≥3	≥3
Minimum capacity charge per object	N/A	N/A	128KB	128KB	128KB	40KB	40KB
Minimum storage duration charge	N/A	N/A	30 days	30 days	90 days	90 days	180 days
Retrieval fee	N/A	N/A	Per GB retrieved	Per GB retrieved	Per GB retrieved	Per GB retrieved	Per GB retrieved
First byte latency	milliseconds	milliseconds	milliseconds	milliseconds	milliseconds	minutes or hours	hours

When you successfully upload a file to S3 you receive a HTTP 200 code.

S3 is a persistent, highly durable data store.

Persistent data stores are non-volatile storage systems that retain data when powered off.

This contrasts with transient data stores and ephemeral data stores which lose the data when powered off.

The following table provides a description of persistent, transient, and ephemeral data stores and which AWS service to use:

Storage Type	Description	Examples
Persistent Data Store	Data is durable and sticks around after reboots, restarts, or power cycles	S3, Glacier, EBS, EFS
Transient Data Store	Data is just temporarily stored and passed along to another process or persistent store	SQS, SNS

| Ephemeral Data Store | Data is lost when the system is stopped | EC2 Instance Store, Memcached |

Bucket names must follow a set of rules:

- Names must be unique across all of AWS.
- Names must be 3 to 63 characters in length.
- Names can only contain lowercase letters, numbers, and hyphens.
- Names cannot be formatted as an IP address.

Objects consist of:

- Key (name of the object).
- Value (data made up of a sequence of bytes).
- Version ID (used for versioning).
- Metadata (data about the data that is stored).

Subresources:

- Access control lists.
- Torrent.

Object sharing – the ability to make any object publicly available via a URL.

Lifecycle management – set rules to transfer objects between storage classes at defined time intervals.

Versioning – automatically keep multiple versions of an object (when enabled).

Encryption can be enabled for bucket.

Data is secured using ACLs and bucket policies.

Charges:

- Storage.
- Requests.
- Storage management pricing.
- Data transfer pricing.
- Transfer acceleration.

When you create a bucket, you need to select the region where it will be created.

It is a best practice to create buckets in regions that are physically closest to your users to reduce latency.

Additional capabilities offered by Amazon S3 include:

Additional S3 Capability	How it Works
Transfer Acceleration	Speed up data uploads using CloudFront in reverse
Requester Pays	The requester rather than the bucket owner pays for requests and data transfer
Tags	Assign tags to objects to use in costing, billing, security etc.

Events	Trigger notifications to SNS, SQS, or Lambda when certain events happen in your bucket
Static Web Hosting	Simple and massively scalable static website hosting
BitTorrent	Use the BitTorrent protocol to retrieve any publicly available object by automatically generating a .torrent file

AWS SNOWBALL

With AWS Snowball (Snowball), you can transfer hundreds of terabytes or petabytes of data between your on-premises data centers and Amazon Simple Storage Service (Amazon S3).

Uses a secure storage device for physical transportation.

AWS Snowball Client is software that is installed on a local computer and is used to identify, compress, encrypt, and transfer data.

Uses 256-bit encryption (managed with the AWS KMS) and tamper-resistant enclosures with TPM.

The table below describes the AWS Snow offerings at a high-level:

Service	What it Is
AWS Snowball	Bulk data transfer, edge storage, and edge compute
AWS Snowmobile	A literal shipping container full of storage (up to 100PB) and a truck to transport it
AWS Snowcone	The smallest device in the range that is best suited for outside the data center

Snowball can import to S3 or export from S3.

Import/export is when you send your own disks into AWS – this is being deprecated in favor of Snowball.

Snowball must be ordered from and returned to the same region.

To speed up data transfer it is recommended to run simultaneous instances of the AWS Snowball Client in multiple terminals and transfer small files as batches.

AMAZON ELASTIC BLOCK STORE (EBS)

Amazon Elastic Block Store (Amazon EBS) provides persistent block storage volumes for use with Amazon EC2 instances in the AWS Cloud.

Each Amazon EBS volume is automatically replicated within its Availability Zone to protect you from component failure, offering high availability and durability.

Amazon EBS volumes offer the consistent and low-latency performance needed to run your workloads. With Amazon EBS, you can scale your usage up or down within minutes – all while paying a low price for only what you provision.

The following EBS volumes appear most often on the AWS exams:

Volume Type	EBS Provisioned IOPS SSD (io1/io2)	EBS General Purpose SSD (gp2/gp3)	Throughput Optimized HDD (st1)	Cold HDD (sc1)
Short Description	Highest performance SSD volume designed for latency-sensitive transactional workloads	General Purpose SSD volume that balances price performance for a wide variety of transactional workloads	Low-cost HDD volume, designed for frequently accessed. Throughput intensive workloads	Lowest cost HDD volume designed for less frequently accessed workloads
Use Cases	I/O-intensive NoSQL and relational databases	Boot volumes, low-latency interactive apps, dev & test	Big-data, data warehouses, log processing	Colder data requiring fewer scans per day
Volume Size	4 GiB - 16 TiB	1 GiB - 16 TiB	125 GB – 16 TiB	125 GB – 16 TiB
Max IOPS** / Volume	64,000	16,000	500	250
Max Throughput***Volume	1,000 MiB/s	250 MiB/s (gp2) 1000 MiB/s (gp3)	500 MiB/s	250 MiB/s
Can be boot volume?	Yes	Yes	No	No
EBS Multi-attach	Supported	Not Supported	Not Supported	Not Supported

EBS volume data persists independently of the life of the instance.

EBS volumes do not need to be attached to an instance.

You can attach multiple EBS volumes to an instance.

You cannot attach an EBS volume to multiple instances (use Elastic File Store instead).

EBS volumes must be in the same AZ as the instances they are attached to.

Termination protection is turned off by default and must be manually enabled (keeps the volume/data when the instance is terminated).

Root EBS volumes are deleted on termination by default.

Extra non-boot volumes are not deleted on termination by default.

The behavior can be changed by altering the "DeleteOnTermination" attribute.

EBS Snapshots:

- Snapshots capture a point-in-time state of an instance.
- Snapshots are stored on S3.
- Does not provide granular backup (not a replacement for backup software).
- If you make periodic snapshots of a volume, the snapshots are incremental, which means that only the blocks on the device that have changed after your last snapshot are saved in the new snapshot.
- Even though snapshots are saved incrementally, the snapshot deletion process is designed so that you need to retain only the most recent snapshot to restore the volume.
- Snapshots can only be accessed through the EC2 APIs.
- EBS volumes are AZ specific, but snapshots are region specific.

© 2023 Digital Cloud Training

INSTANCE STORE VOLUMES

Instance store volumes are high performance local disks that are physically attached to the host computer on which an EC2 instance runs.

Instance stores are ephemeral which means the data is lost when powered off (non-persistent).

Instances stores are ideal for temporary storage of information that changes frequently, such as buffers, caches, or scratch data.

Instance store volume root devices are created from AMI templates stored on S3.

Instance store volumes cannot be detached/reattached.

AMAZON ELASTIC FILE SYSTEM (EFS)

EFS is a fully managed service that makes it easy to set up and scale file storage in the Amazon Cloud.

Good for big data and analytics, media processing workflows, content management, web serving, home directories etc.

EFS uses the NFS protocol.

Pay for what you use (no pre-provisioning required).

Can scale up to petabytes.

EFS is elastic and grows and shrinks as you add and remove data.

Can concurrently connect 1 to 1000s of EC2 instances, from multiple AZs.

A file system can be accessed concurrently from all AZs in the region where it is located.

By default, you can create up to 10 file systems per account.

On-premises access can be enabled via Direct Connect or AWS VPN.

Can choose General Purpose or Max I/O (both SSD).

The VPC of the connecting instance must have DNS hostnames enabled.

EFS provides a file system interface, file system access semantics (such as strong consistency and file locking).

Data is stored across multiple AZs within a region.

Read after write consistency.

Need to create mount targets and choose AZs to include (recommended to include all AZ's).

Instances can be behind an ELB.

There are two performance modes:

- "General Purpose" performance mode is appropriate for most file systems.
- "Max I/O" performance mode is optimized for applications where tens, hundreds, or thousands of EC2 instances are accessing the file system.

Amazon EFS is designed to burst to allow high throughput levels for periods of time.

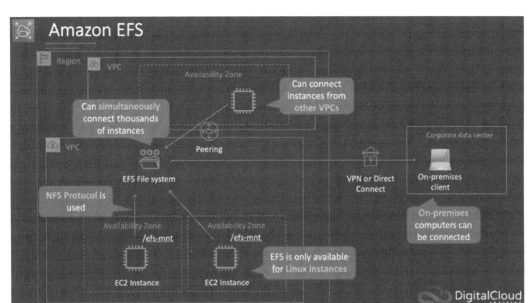

AWS STORAGE GATEWAY

AWS Storage Gateway is a hybrid cloud storage service that gives you on-premises access to virtually unlimited cloud storage.

Customers use Storage Gateway to simplify storage management and reduce costs for key hybrid cloud storage use cases.

These include moving backups to the cloud, using on-premises file shares backed by cloud storage, and providing low latency access to data in AWS for on-premises applications.

To support these use cases, Storage Gateway offers three different types of gateways:

- File Gateway – provides file system interfaces to on-premises servers.
- Volume Gateway – provides block-based access for on-premises servers.
- Tape Gateway – provides a virtual tape library that is compatible with common backup software (block and file interfaces).

© 2023 Digital Cloud Training

AWS STORAGE QUIZ QUESTIONS

Answers and explanations are provided below after the last question in this section.

Question 1: What is the most cost-effective storage tier for data that is not often accessed, will be retained for 7 years, and needs to be retrievable within 24 hours?

1. Amazon S3 Standard
2. Amazon S3 Glacier
3. Amazon S3 Standard-Infrequent Access
4. Amazon S3 Glacier Deep Archive

Question 2: Which storage classes are available for the Amazon Elastic File System?

1. Standard, Provisioned Throughput
2. Standard, Deep Archive
3. Standard, Infrequent Access Storage
4. Standard, One-Zone IA

Question 3: Amazon S3 is an example of what type of storage system?

1. Object
2. Block
3. File
4. Hybrid

Question 4: With Amazon S3, objects are stored in which type of root-level container?

1. A folder
2. A file-system
3. A bucket
4. A region

Question 5: Amazon Elastic Block Store (EBS) volumes are stored within which construct?

1. A region
2. An edge location
3. A snapshot
4. An availability zone

Question 6: Which storage service can be used on-premises to access cloud storage?

1. Amazon S3 Glacier
2. Amazon Storage Block
3. AWS Storage Gateway
4. AWS Hybrid Service

Question 7: With default settings, what will happen to a root EBS volume when the Amazon EC2 instance is terminated?

1. It will be deleted

2. It will be retained
3. A snapshot will be retained
4. An AMI will be created

Question 8: Which Amazon Machine Image can be used to mount an Amazon Elastic File System (EFS) file system?

1. Microsoft Windows Server 2019 with Containers
2. Microsoft Windows Server 2016 Core
3. Amazon Linux 2 AMI
4. All of the above

Question 9: Which storage device is physically attached to the Amazon EC2 host servers?

1. Amazon Elastic Block Store (EBS) volume
2. Amazon Machine Image (AMI)
3. Instance Store volume
4. Elastic Network Adapter

Question 10: Which Amazon S3 storage class is used for archiving data for long term retention?

1. S3 Standard
2. S3 Intelligent-Tiering
3. S3 One Zone-IA
4. S3 Glacier Deep Archive

Question 11: Which storage service is used by Amazon EC2 instances for the root volume?

1. Amazon Simple Storage Service (S3)
2. Amazon Elastic File System (EFS)
3. Amazon Elastic Block Store (EBS)
4. Amazon Storage Gateway

AWS STORAGE ANSWERS

Question 1: What is the most cost-effective storage tier for data that is not often accessed, will be retained for 7 years, and needs to be retrievable within 24 hours?

1. Amazon S3 Standard
2. Amazon S3 Glacier
3. Amazon S3 Standard-Infrequent Access
4. Amazon S3 Glacier Deep Archive

Answer: 4

Explanation:

1 is incorrect. This is not the most affordable option for long term data storage

2 is incorrect. This is not the most affordable option for long term data storage where retrieval times of 24 hours are acceptable

3 is incorrect. This is not the most affordable option for long term data storage where retrieval times of 24 hours are acceptable

4 is correct. This is the most affordable option for long term data storage where retrieval times of 24 hours are acceptable

Question 2: Which storage classes are available for the Amazon Elastic File System?

1. Standard, Provisioned Throughput
2. Standard, Deep Archive
3. Standard, Infrequent Access Storage
4. Standard, One-Zone IA

Answer: 3

Explanation:

1 is incorrect. Provisioned throughput is not a storage class, it is a way you can get better performance for additional cost

2 is incorrect. Deep Archive is a tier of Glacier storage, not EFS

3 is correct. These are the two storage classes available for EFS

4 is incorrect. One-Zone IA is an Amazon S3 storage class

Question 3: Amazon S3 is an example of what type of storage system?

1. Object
2. Block
3. File
4. Hybrid

Answer: 1

Explanation:

1 is correct. Amazon Simple Storage Service (S3) is an object-based storage system

2 is incorrect. Amazon Simple Storage Service (S3) is not a block-based storage system

3 is incorrect. Amazon Simple Storage Service (S3) is not a file-based storage system

4 is incorrect. Amazon Simple Storage Service (S3) is not a hybrid storage system. An example of a hybrid storage system would be Amazon Storage Gateway

Question 4: With Amazon S3, objects are stored in which type of root-level container?

1. A folder
2. A file-system
3. A bucket
4. A region

Answer: 3

Explanation:

1 is incorrect. You can create folders with Amazon S3 to mimic a hierarchy, but they are not root-level containers

2 is incorrect. Amazon S3 is an object-based storage system, there is no such thing as a file-system

3 is correct. A bucket is the root-level container in Amazon S3. You upload your objects into buckets

4 is incorrect. A region is not the root-level container in Amazon S3. Buckets are created within a region

Question 5: Amazon Elastic Block Store (EBS) volumes are stored within which construct?

1. A region
2. An edge location
3. A snapshot
4. An availability zone

Answer: 4

Explanation:

1 is incorrect. Amazon EBS volumes are not stored within a region. They are stored within another construct that is within a region. Guess again!

2 is incorrect. An edge location is not where you store EBS volumes. Edge Locations are used by the Amazon CloudFront service and will be discussed later in the course

3 is incorrect. You don't store an Amazon EBS volume in a snapshot, you take snapshots of EBS volumes to get point-in-time backups of the data in the volume

4 is correct. Amazon EBS volumes are stored with an availability zone.

Question 6: Which storage service can be used on-premises to access cloud storage?

1. Amazon S3 Glacier
2. Amazon Storage Block
3. AWS Storage Gateway

© 2023 Digital Cloud Training

4. AWS Hybrid Service

Answer: 3

Explanation:

1 is incorrect. Amazon S3 Glacier is a cloud storage solution used for archiving data

2 is incorrect. There's no such thing as "Amazon Storage Block"

3 is correct. AWS Storage Gateway is a hybrid cloud storage service that gives you on-premises access to virtually unlimited cloud storage

4 is incorrect. There's no such thing as "AWS Hybrid Service"

Question 7: With default settings, what will happen to a root EBS volume when the Amazon EC2 instance is terminated?

1. It will be deleted
2. It will be retained
3. A snapshot will be retained
4. An AMI will be created

Answer: 1

Explanation:

1 is correct. With default settings an Amazon EBS root volume will be deleted when the instance is terminated

2 is incorrect. This is, not true with default settings. However, you can configure EBS volumes to be retained by changing the "Delete on termination" attribute

3 is incorrect. A snapshot is not automatically created when an instance is terminated

4 is incorrect. An AMI will not be created

Question 8: Which Amazon Machine Image can be used to mount an Amazon Elastic File System (EFS) file system?

1. Microsoft Windows Server 2019 with Containers
2. Microsoft Windows Server 2016 Core
3. Amazon Linux 2 AMI
4. All of the above

Answer: 3

Explanation:

1 is incorrect. You cannot use Microsoft Windows AMIs with Amazon EFS

2 is incorrect. You cannot use Microsoft Windows AMIs with Amazon EFS

3 is correct. Only Linux AMIs can be used with Amazon EFS

4 is incorrect. You cannot use Microsoft Windows AMIs with Amazon EFS

Question 9: Which storage device is physically attached to the Amazon EC2 host servers?

1. Amazon Elastic Block Store (EBS) volume

2. Amazon Machine Image (AMI)
3. Instance Store volume
4. Elastic Network Adapter

Answer: 3

Explanation:

1 is incorrect. Amazon EBS volumes are attached over a network, they are not physically attached to the EC2 host servers

2 is incorrect. An AMI is used to launch an instance, it is not a storage device

3 is correct. Instance store volumes are physically attached to EC2 host servers. They are ephemeral storage which means the data is lost when powered off

4 is incorrect. An ENA is not a storage device

Question 10: Which Amazon S3 storage class is used for archiving data for long term retention?

1. S3 Standard
2. S3 Intelligent-Tiering
3. S3 One Zone-IA
4. S3 Glacier Deep Archive

Answer: 4

Explanation:

1 is incorrect. S3 Standard is durable, immediately available, frequently accessed storage

2 is incorrect. S3 Intelligent-Tiering automatically moves data to the most cost-effective tier

3 is incorrect. S3 One Zone-IA is lower cost storage for infrequently accessed data with less resilience

4 is correct. S3 Glacier Deep Archive is the lowest cost storage class for long term retention

Question 11: Which storage service is used by Amazon EC2 instances for the root volume?

1. Amazon Simple Storage Service (S3)
2. Amazon Elastic File System (EFS)
3. Amazon Elastic Block Store (EBS)
4. Amazon Storage Gateway

Answer: 3

Explanation:

1 is incorrect. Amazon S3 is an object-based storage system and is not used for EC2 root volumes

2 is incorrect. Amazon Elastic File System (EFS) is a file-based storage service. You can mount EFS filesystems to an EC2 instance, but you cannot use them for root volumes

3 is correct. Amazon Elastic Block Store (EBS) is used for the root volume on EBS-backed instances

4 is incorrect. Amazon Storage Gateway is a storage solution used for hybrid storage between on-premises and AWS Cloud

AWS NETWORKING

This article covers AWS Networking which is a key technology area in the Cloud Practitioner exam blueprint

AMAZON VIRTUAL PRIVATE CLOUD (VPC)

A virtual private cloud (VPC) is a virtual network dedicated to your AWS account.

Analogous to having your own DC inside AWS.

It is logically isolated from other virtual networks in the AWS Cloud.

Provides complete control over the virtual networking environment including selection of IP ranges, creation of subnets, and configuration of route tables and gateways.

You can launch your AWS resources, such as Amazon EC2 instances, into your VPC.

When you create a VPC, you must specify a range of IPv4 addresses for the VPC in the form of a Classless Inter-Domain Routing (CIDR) block; for example, 10.0.0.0/16.

This is the primary CIDR block for your VPC.

A VPC spans all the Availability Zones in the region.

You have full control over who has access to the AWS resources inside your VPC.

You can create your own IP address ranges, and create subnets, route tables and network gateways.

When you first create your AWS account a default VPC is created for you in each AWS region.

A default VPC is created in each region with a subnet in each AZ.

By default, you can create up to 5 VPCs per region.

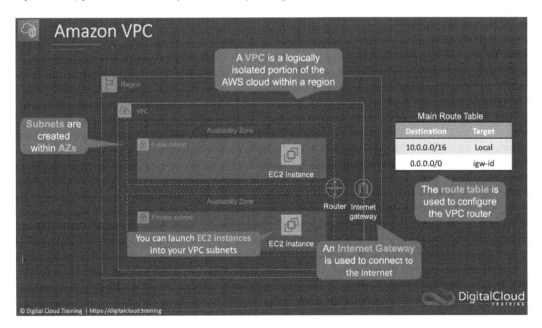

© 2023 Digital Cloud Training

You can define dedicated tenancy for a VPC to ensure instances are launched on dedicated hardware (overrides the configuration specified at launch).

A default VPC is automatically created for each AWS account the first time Amazon EC2 resources are provisioned.

The default VPC has all-public subnets.

Public subnets are subnets that have:

- "Auto-assign public IPv4 address" set to "Yes".
- The subnet route table has an attached Internet Gateway.

Instances in the default VPC always have both a public and private IP address.

AZs names are mapped to different zones for different users (i.e. the AZ "ap-southeast-2a" may map to a different physical zone for a different user).

Components of a VPC:

- **A Virtual Private Cloud**: A logically isolated virtual network in the AWS cloud. You define a VPC's IP address space from ranges you select.
- **Subnet**: A segment of a VPC's IP address range where you can place groups of isolated resources (maps to an AZ, 1:1).
- **Internet Gateway**: The Amazon VPC side of a connection to the public Internet.
- **NAT Gateway**: A highly available, managed Network Address Translation (NAT) service for your resources in a private subnet to access the Internet.
- **Hardware VPN Connection**: A hardware-based VPN connection between your Amazon VPC and your datacenter, home network, or co-location facility.
- **Virtual Private Gateway**: The Amazon VPC side of a VPN connection.
- **Customer Gateway**: Your side of a VPN connection.
- **Router**: Routers interconnect subnets and direct traffic between Internet gateways, virtual private gateways, NAT gateways, and subnets.
- **Peering Connection**: A peering connection enables you to route traffic via private IP addresses between two peered VPCs.
- **VPC Endpoints**: Enables private connectivity to services hosted in AWS, from within your VPC without using an Internet Gateway, VPN, Network Address Translation (NAT) devices, or firewall proxies.
- **Egress-only Internet Gateway**: A stateful gateway to provide egress only access for IPv6 traffic from the VPC to the Internet.

Options for securely connecting to a VPC are:

- AWS managed VPN – fast to setup.
- Direct Connect – high bandwidth, low-latency but takes weeks to months to setup.
- VPN CloudHub – used for connecting multiple sites to AWS.
- Software VPN – use 3rd party software.

An Elastic Network Interface (ENI) is a logical networking component that represents a NIC.

ENIs can be attached and detached from EC2 instances, and the configuration of the ENI will be maintained.

Flow Logs capture information about the IP traffic going to and from network interfaces in a VPC.

Flow log data is stored using Amazon CloudWatch Logs.

Flow logs can be created at the following levels:

- VPC.
- Subnet.
- Network interface.

Peering connections can be created with VPCs in different regions (available in most regions now).

SUBNETS

After creating a VPC, you can add one or more subnets in each Availability Zone.

When you create a subnet, you specify the CIDR block for the subnet, which is a subset of the VPC CIDR block.

Each subnet must reside entirely within one Availability Zone and cannot span zones.

Types of subnets:

- If a subnet's traffic is routed to an internet gateway, the subnet is known as a public subnet.
- If a subnet doesn't have a route to the internet gateway, the subnet is known as a private subnet.
- If a subnet doesn't have a route to the internet gateway, but has its traffic routed to a virtual private gateway for a VPN connection, the subnet is known as a VPN-only subnet.

An Internet Gateway is a horizontally scaled, redundant, and highly available VPC component that allows communication between instances in your VPC and the internet.

FIREWALLS

Network Access Control Lists (ACLs) provide a firewall/security layer at the subnet level.

Security Groups provide a firewall/security layer at the instance level.

The table below describes some differences between Security Groups and Network ACLs:

Security Group	Network ACL
Operates at the instance (interface) level	Operates at the subnet level
Supports allow rules only	Supports allow and deny rules
Stateful	Stateless
Evaluates all rules	Processes rules in order
Applies to an instance only if associated with a group	Automatically applies to all instances in the subnets its associated with

VPC WIZARD

The VPC Wizard can be used to create the following four configurations:

VPC with a Single Public Subnet:

- Your instances run in a private, isolated section of the AWS cloud with direct access to the Internet.
- Network access control lists and security groups can be used to provide strict control over inbound and outbound network traffic to your instances.
- Creates a /16 network with a /24 subnet. Public subnet instances use Elastic IPs or Public IPs to access the Internet.

VPC with Public and Private Subnets:

- In addition to containing a public subnet, this configuration adds a private subnet whose instances are not addressable from the Internet.
- Instances in the private subnet can establish outbound connections to the Internet via the public subnet using Network Address Translation (NAT).
- Creates a /16 network with two /24 subnets.
- Public subnet instances use Elastic IPs to access the Internet.
- Private subnet instances access the Internet via Network Address Translation (NAT).

VPC with Public and Private Subnets and Hardware VPN Access:

- This configuration adds an IPsec Virtual Private Network (VPN) connection between your Amazon VPC and your data center – effectively extending your data center to the cloud while also providing direct access to the Internet for public subnet instances in your Amazon VPC.
- Creates a /16 network with two /24 subnets.
- One subnet is directly connected to the Internet while the other subnet is connected to your corporate network via an IPsec VPN tunnel.

VPC with a Private Subnet Only and Hardware VPN Access:

- Your instances run in a private, isolated section of the AWS cloud with a private subnet whose instances are not addressable from the Internet.
- You can connect this private subnet to your corporate data center via an IPsec Virtual Private Network (VPN) tunnel.
- Creates a /16 network with a /24 subnet and provisions an IPsec VPN tunnel between your Amazon VPC and your corporate network.

NAT INSTANCES

NAT instances are managed **by** you.

Used to enable private subnet instances to access the Internet.

When creating NAT instances always disable the source/destination check on the instance.

NAT instances must be in a single public subnet.

NAT instances need to be assigned to security groups.

NAT Gateways

NAT gateways are managed **for** you by AWS.

NAT gateways are highly available in each AZ into which they are deployed.

They are preferred by enterprises.

Can scale automatically up to 45Gbps.

No need to patch.

Not associated with any security groups.

The table below describes some differences between NAT instances and NAT gateways:

NAT Instance	NAT Gateway
Managed by you (e.g. software updates)	Managed by AWS
Scale up (instance type) manually and use enhanced networking	Elastic scalability up to 45 Gbps
No high availability – scripted/auto-scaled HA possible using multiple NATs in multiple subnets	Provides automatic high availability within an AZ and can be placed in multiple AZs
Need to assign Security Group	No Security Groups
Can use as a bastion host	Cannot access through SSH

AWS DIRECT CONNECT (DX)

AWS Direct Connect is a network service that provides an alternative to using the Internet to connect a customer's on-premises sites to AWS.

Data is transmitted through a private network connection between AWS and a customer's data center or corporate network.

Benefits of Direct Connect:

- Reduce cost when using large volumes of traffic.
- Increase reliability (predictable performance).
- Increase bandwidth (predictable bandwidth).
- Decrease latency.

Each AWS Direct Connect connection can be configured with one or more virtual interfaces (VIFs).

Public VIFs allow access to public services such as S3, EC2, and DynamoDB.

Private VIFs allow access to your VPC.

From Direct Connect you can connect to all AZs **within the Region.**

You can establish IPSec connections over public VIFs to remote regions.

Direct Connect is charged by port hours and data transfer.

Available in 1Gbps and 10Gbps.

Speeds of 50Mbps, 100Mbps, 200Mbps, 300Mbps, 400Mbps, and 500Mbps can be purchased through AWS Direct Connect Partners.

Each connection consists of a single dedicated connection between ports on the customer router and an Amazon router.

for HA you must have 2 DX connections – can be active/active or active/standby.

Route tables need to be updated to point to a Direct Connect connection.

AWS GLOBAL ACCELERATOR

AWS Global Accelerator is a service that improves the availability and performance of applications with local or global users.

It provides static IP addresses that act as a fixed entry point to application endpoints in a single or multiple AWS Regions, such as Application Load Balancers, Network Load Balancers or EC2 instances.

Uses the AWS global network to optimize the path from users to applications, improving the performance of TCP and UDP traffic.

AWS Global Accelerator continually monitors the health of application endpoints and will detect an unhealthy endpoint and redirect traffic to healthy endpoints in less than 1 minute.

DETAILS AND BENEFITS

Uses redundant (two) static anycast IP addresses in different network zones (A and B).

The redundant pair are globally advertised.

Uses AWS Edge Locations – addresses are announced from multiple edge locations at the same time.

Addresses are associated to regional AWS resources or endpoints.

AWS Global Accelerator's IP addresses serve as the frontend interface of applications.

Intelligent traffic distribution: Routes connections to the closest point of presence for applications.

Targets can be Amazon EC2 instances or Elastic Load Balancers (ALB and NLB).

By using the static IP addresses, you don't need to make any client-facing changes or update DNS records as you modify or replace endpoints.

The addresses are assigned to your accelerator for as long as it exists, even if you disable the accelerator and it no longer accepts or routes traffic.

AWS OUTPOSTS

AWS Outposts is a fully managed service that offers the same AWS infrastructure, AWS services, APIs, and tools to virtually any datacenter, co-location space, or on-premises facility for a truly consistent hybrid experience.

AWS Outposts is ideal for workloads that require low latency access to on-premises systems, local data processing, data residency, and migration of applications with local system interdependencies.

AWS compute, storage, database, and other services run locally on Outposts, and you can access the full range of AWS services available in the Region to build, manage, and scale your on-premises applications using familiar AWS services and tools.

Outposts is available as a 42U rack that can scale from 1 rack to 96 racks to create pools of compute and storage capacity.

Services you can run on AWS Outposts include:

- Amazon EC2.
- Amazon EBS.
- Amazon S3.
- Amazon VPC.
- Amazon ECS/EKS.
- Amazon RDS.
- Amazon EMR.

© 2023 Digital Cloud Training

AWS NETWORKING QUIZ QUESTIONS

Answers and explanations are provided below after the last question in this section.

Question 1: What is the scope of an Amazon VPC?

1. A data center
2. A region
3. An availability zone
4. A subnet

Question 2: Which type of firewall operates at the instance level?

1. A security group
2. A network access control list (NACL)
3. A route table
4. A NAT Gateway

Question 3: How can an organization create a private hybrid cloud connection between their on-premises data center and the AWS Cloud?

1. AWS managed VPN
2. VPN CloudHub
3. Software VPN
4. AWS Direct Connect

Question 4: Which type of public IP address is retained when the instance is stopped?

1. Public IP address
2. Private IP address
3. Elastic IP address
4. Local IP address

Question 5: Which AWS-managed network service can be used to enable Internet connectivity for EC2 instances in private subnets?

1. NAT Instance
2. NAT Gateway
3. Internet Gateway
4. Network ACL

Question 6: A company needs a network connection to the AWS cloud with predictable performance. What should they use?

1. AWS managed VPN
2. AWS Direct Connect
3. VPN CloudHub
4. VPC Peering

Question 7: With Amazon Virtual Private Cloud (VPC) what must you pay for?

1. Internet Gateway
2. Route Table
3. Security Group
4. VPN Connection

AWS NETWORKING ANSWERS

Question 1: What is the scope of an Amazon VPC?

1. A data center
2. A region
3. An availability zone
4. A subnet

Answer: 2

Explanation:

> **1 is incorrect.** The scope of a VPC is not a data center. AWS never talk in terms of data centers as these are transparent to the user

> **2 is correct.** An Amazon VPC is created within a region. You can create multiple VPCs within a region and there is a default VPC created in every AWS region by default

> **3 is incorrect.** You do not create VPC's within availability zones. AZs are actually constructs to which you assign subnets within your VPC

> **4 is incorrect.** A subnet is assigned to an availability zone, you don't create a VPC in a subnet

Question 2: Which type of firewall operates at the instance level?

1. A security group
2. A network access control list (NACL)
3. A route table
4. A NAT Gateway

Answer: 1

Explanation:

> **1 is correct.** Security groups are considered to be instance-level firewalls

> **2 is incorrect.** A network access control list or NACL is a subnet-level firewall

> **3 is incorrect.** A route table is not a firewall. It is used to direct network traffic

> **4 is incorrect.** A NAT Gateway is not a firewall. It is used to provide Internet access to EC2 instances in private subnets

Question 3: How can an organization create a private hybrid cloud connection between their on-premises data center and the AWS Cloud?

1. AWS managed VPN
2. VPN CloudHub
3. Software VPN
4. AWS Direct Connect

Answer: 4

Explanation:

1 is incorrect. A virtual private network (VPN) is a connection over the public Internet and is therefore not considered private

2 is incorrect. A virtual private network (VPN) is a connection over the public Internet and is therefore not considered private

3 is incorrect. A virtual private network (VPN) is a connection over the public Internet and is therefore not considered private

4 is correct. AWS Direct Connect is a private network connection to the AWS Cloud. It provides high bandwidth and low latency with reliable performance

Question 4: Which type of public IP address is retained when the instance is stopped?

1. Public IP address
2. Private IP address
3. Elastic IP address
5. Local IP address

Answer: 3

Explanation:

1 is incorrect. Public IP addresses are lost when the instance is stopped

2 is incorrect. A private IP address is not a public IP address

3 is correct. With Elastic IP addresses, the address is retained when the instance is stopped. Remember that you do pay for unused Elastic IP addresses

4 is incorrect. This is not a type of Public IP address

Question 5: Which AWS-managed network service can be used to enable Internet connectivity for EC2 instances in private subnets?

1. NAT Instance
2. NAT Gateway
3. Internet Gateway
4. Network ACL

Answer: 2

Explanation:

1 is incorrect. A NAT instance is an EC2 instance managed by you that can be used for enabling instance in private subnets to access the Internet

2 is correct. A NAT Gateway is an AWS managed service that can be used for enabling instance in private subnets to access the Internet

3 is incorrect. An Internet Gateway is attached to a VPC to enable Internet connectivity. However, you need a NAT Instance or NAT Gateway to enable instance in private subnets to access the Internet using the Internet Gateway

4 is incorrect. A network ACL is a subnet-level firewall

Question 6: A company needs a network connection to the AWS cloud with predictable

performance. What should they use?

1. AWS managed VPN
2. AWS Direct Connect
3. VPN CloudHub
4. VPC Peering

Answer: 2

Explanation:

> **1 is incorrect.** Because a VPN uses the public Internet, it doesn't offer predictable performance

> **2 is correct.** AWS Direct Connect is a private network connection and offers predictable performance

> **3 is incorrect.** Because a VPN uses the public Internet, it doesn't offer predictable performance

> **4 is incorrect.** VPC Peering is a method of connecting two VPCs together, not for connecting into AWS from an organization

Question 7: With Amazon Virtual Private Cloud (VPC) what must you pay for?

1. Internet Gateway
2. Route Table
3. Security Group
4. VPN Connection

Answer: 4

Explanation:

> **1 is incorrect.** You do not need to pay for Internet Gateways

> **2 is incorrect.** You do not need to pay for Route Tables

> **3 is incorrect.** You do not need to pay for Security Groups

> **4 is correct.** You do need to pay for VPN connections

AWS DATABASES

This article covers AWS Databases for the AWS Cloud Practitioner exam. This is one of the key technology areas covered in the exam blueprint.

USE CASES FOR DIFFERENT DATABASE TYPES

The table below provides guidance on the typical use cases for several AWS database/data store services:

Data Store	When to Use
Database on EC2	<ul><li>Full control over instance and database</li><li>Preferred DB not available under RDS</li></ul>
Amazon RDS	<ul><li>Need traditional relational database for OLTP</li><li>Your data is well-formed and structured</li><li>Existing applications requiring RDBMS</li></ul>
Amazon DynamoDB	<ul><li>Name/value pair data</li><li>Unpredictable data structure</li><li>In-memory performance with persistence</li><li>High I/O needs</li><li>Require dynamic scaling</li></ul>
Amazon RedShift	<ul><li>Data warehouse for large volumes of aggregated data</li><li>Primarily OLAP workloads</li></ul>
Amazon Neptune	<ul><li>Relationships between objects are of high value</li></ul>
Amazon ElastiCache	<ul><li>Fast temporary storage for small amounts of data</li><li>Highly volatile data (non-persistent)</li></ul>
Amazon S3	<ul><li>Binary large objects (BLOBs)</li><li>Static websites</li></ul>

We'll now cover several of these database types that may come up on the exam.

AMAZON RELATIONAL DATABASE SERVICE (RDS)

Amazon Relational Database Service (Amazon RDS) is a managed service that makes it easy to set up, operate, and scale a relational database in the cloud.

Relational databases are known as Structured Query Language (SQL) databases.

Non-relational databases are known as NoSQL databases.

RDS is an Online Transaction Processing (OLTP) type of database.

RDS features and benefits:

- SQL type of database.

- Can be used to perform complex queries and joins.
- Easy to setup, highly available, fault tolerant, and scalable.
- Used when data is clearly defined.
- Common use cases include online stores and banking systems.

Amazon RDS supports the following database engines:

- SQL Server.
- Oracle.
- MySQL Server.
- PostgreSQL.
- Aurora.
- MariaDB.

Aurora is Amazon's proprietary database.

RDS is a fully managed service and you do not have access to the underlying EC2 instance (no root access).

The RDS service includes the following:

- Security and patching of the DB instances.
- Automated backup for the DB instances.
- Software updates for the DB engine.
- Easy scaling for storage and compute.
- Multi-AZ option with synchronous replication.
- Automatic failover for Multi-AZ option.
- Read replicas option for read heavy workloads.

A DB instance is a database environment in the cloud with the compute and storage resources you specify.

Encryption:

- You can encrypt your Amazon RDS instances and snapshots at rest by enabling the encryption option for your Amazon RDS DB instance.
- Encryption at rest is supported for all DB types and uses AWS KMS.
- You cannot encrypt an existing DB, you need to create a snapshot, copy it, encrypt the copy, then build an encrypted DB from the snapshot.

DB Subnet Groups:

- A DB subnet group is a collection of subnets (typically private) that you create in a VPC and that you then designate for your DB instances.
- Each DB subnet group should have subnets in at least two Availability Zones in each region.
- It is recommended to configure a subnet group with subnets in each AZ (even for standalone instances).

AWS Charge for:

- DB instance hours (partial hours are charged as full hours).
- Storage GB/month.
- I/O requests/month – for magnetic storage.

- Provisioned IOPS/month – for RDS provisioned IOPS SSD.
- Egress data transfer.
- Backup storage (DB backups and manual snapshots).

Scalability:

- You can only scale RDS up (compute and storage).
- You cannot decrease the allocated storage for an RDS instance.
- You can scale storage and change the storage type for all DB engines except MS SQL.

RDS provides multi-AZ for disaster recovery which provides fault tolerance across availability zones:

- Multi-AZ RDS creates a replica in another AZ and synchronously replicates to it (DR only).
- There is an option to choose multi-AZ during the launch wizard.
- AWS recommends the use of provisioned IOPS storage for multi-AZ RDS DB instances.
- Each AZ runs on its own physically distinct, independent infrastructure, and is engineered to be highly reliable.
- You cannot choose which AZ in the region will be chosen to create the standby DB instance.

Read Replicas – provide improved performance for reads:

- Read replicas are used for read heavy DBs and replication is asynchronous.
- Read replicas are for workload sharing and offloading.
- Read replicas provide read-only DR.
- Read replicas are created from a snapshot of the master instance.
- Must have automated backups enabled on the primary (retention period > 0).

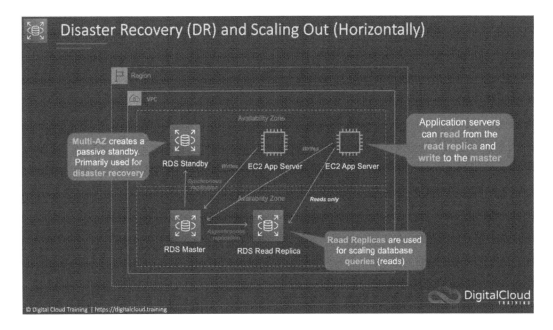

© 2023 Digital Cloud Training

AMAZON DYNAMODB

Amazon DynamoDB is a fully managed NoSQL database service that provides fast and predictable performance with seamless scalability.

Dynamo DB features and benefits:

- NoSQL type of database (non-relational).
- Fast, highly available, and fully managed.
- Used when data is fluid and can change.
- Common use cases include social networks and web analytics.

Push button scaling means that you can scale the DB at any time without incurring downtime.

SSD based and uses limited indexing on attributes for performance.

DynamoDB is a Web service that uses HTTP over SSL (HTTPS) as a transport and JSON as a message serialization format.

Amazon DynamoDB stores three geographically distributed replicas of each table to enable high availability and data durability.

Data is synchronously replicated across 3 facilities (AZs) in a region.

Cross-region replication allows you to replicate across regions:

- Amazon DynamoDB global tables provides a fully managed solution for deploying a multi-region, multi-master database.
- When you create a global table, you specify the AWS regions where you want the table to be available.
- DynamoDB performs all the necessary tasks to create identical tables in these regions and propagate ongoing data changes to all of them.

Provides low read and write latency.

Scale storage and throughput up or down as needed without code changes or downtime.

DynamoDB is schema-less.

DynamoDB can be used for storing session state.

Provides two read models.

Eventually consistent reads (Default):

- The eventual consistency option maximizes your read throughput (best read performance).
- An eventually consistent read might not reflect the results of a recently completed write.
- Consistency across all copies reached within 1 second.

Strongly consistent reads:

- A strongly consistent read returns a result that reflects all writes that received a successful response prior to the read (faster consistency).

Amazon DynamoDB Accelerator (DAX) is a fully managed, highly available, in-memory cache for DynamoDB that delivers up to a 10x performance improvement – from milliseconds to microseconds – even at millions of requests per second.

AMAZON REDSHIFT

Amazon Redshift is a fast, fully managed data warehouse that makes it simple and cost-effective to analyze all your data using standard SQL and existing Business Intelligence (BI) tools.

RedShift is a SQL based data warehouse used for **analytics** applications.

RedShift is a relational database that is used for Online Analytics Processing (OLAP) use cases.

RedShift is used for running complex analytic queries against petabytes of structured data, using sophisticated query optimization, columnar storage on high-performance local disks, and massively parallel query execution.

RedShift is ideal for **processing** large amounts of data for business intelligence.

RedShift is 10x faster than a traditional SQL DB.

RedShift uses columnar data storage:

- Data is stored sequentially in columns instead of rows.
- Columnar based DB is ideal for data warehousing and analytics.
- Requires fewer I/Os which greatly enhances performance.

RedShift provides advanced compression:

- Data is stored sequentially in columns which allows for much better performance and less storage space.
- RedShift automatically selects the compression scheme.

RedShift uses replication and continuous backups to enhance availability and improve durability and can automatically recover from component and node failures.

RedShift always keeps three copies of your data:

- The original.
- A replica on compute nodes (within the cluster).
- A backup copy on S3.

RedShift provides continuous/incremental backups:

- Multiple copies within a cluster.
- Continuous and incremental backups to S3.
- Continuous and incremental backups across regions.
- Streaming restore.

RedShift provides fault tolerance for the following failures:

- Disk failures.
- Nodes failures.
- Network failures.
- AZ/region level disasters.

AMAZON ELASTICACHE

ElastiCache is a web service that makes it easy to deploy and run Memcached or Redis protocol-compliant server nodes in the cloud.

The in-memory caching provided by ElastiCache can be used to significantly improve latency and throughput for many read-heavy application workloads or compute-intensive workloads.

Best for scenarios where the DB load is based on Online Analytics Processing (OLAP) transactions.

The following table describes a few typical use cases for ElastiCache:

Use Case	Benefit
Web session store	In cases with load-balanced web servers, store web session information in Redis so if a server is lost, the session info is not lost, and another web server can pick it up
Database caching	Use Memcached in front of AWS RDS to cache popular queries to offload work from RDS and return results faster to users
Leaderboards	Use Redis to provide a live leaderboard for millions of users of your mobile app
Streaming data dashboards	Provide a landing spot for streaming sensor data on the factory floor, providing live real-time dashboard displays

ElastiCache EC2 nodes cannot be accessed from the Internet, nor can they be accessed by EC2 instances in other VPCs.

Can be on-demand or reserved instances too (but not Spot instances).

ElastiCache can be used for storing session state.

There are two types of ElastiCache engine:

- Memcached – simplest model, can run large nodes with multiple cores/threads, can be scaled in and out, can cache objects such as DBs.
- Redis – complex model, supports encryption, master / slave replication, cross AZ (HA), automatic failover and backup/restore.

AMAZON EMR

Amazon EMR is a web service that enables businesses, researchers, data analysts, and developers to process vast amounts of data easily and cost-effectively.

EMR utilizes a hosted Hadoop framework running on Amazon EC2 and Amazon S3.

Managed Hadoop framework for processing huge amounts of data.

Also support Apache Spark, HBase, Presto and Flink.

Most commonly used for log analysis, financial analysis, or extract, translate and loading (ETL) activities.

AWS DATABASES QUIZ QUESTIONS

Answers and explanations are provided below after the last question in this section.

Question 1: Amazon Relational Database Service (RDS) is an example of what type of database?

1. Online transaction processing (OLTP)
2. Online analytics processing (OLAP)
3. No-SQL
4. Data warehouse

Question 2: Which AWS database service offers seamless horizontal scaling?

1. Amazon RDS
2. Amazon RedShift
3. Amazon DynamoDB
4. Database on Amazon EC2

Question 3: How can fault tolerance be added to an Amazon RDS database?

1. Using read replicas
2. Using multi-AZ
3. Using Global Replicas
4. Using EBS snapshots

Question 4: How can an organization enable microsecond latency for a DynamoDB database?

1. Using Amazon ElastiCache
2. Using DynamoDB Auto Scaling
3. Using Read Replicas
4. Using DynamoDB Accelerator (DAX)

Question 5: Which AWS database service is a relational, data warehouse?

1. Amazon RedShift
2. Amazon RDS Aurora
3. Amazon DynamoDB
4. Amazon ElastiCache

Question 6: Why might an organization decide to move an on-premises database to Amazon RDS?

1. To reduce operational overhead
2. To increase flexibility
3. To eliminate the need to patch management
4. To benefit from seamless scalability

Question 7: How do you increase the capacity of an Amazon RDS database?

1. Scaling horizontally, by adding instances
2. Scaling horizontally, by adding RCUs/WCUs
3. Scaling vertically, by changing instance type
4. Scaling vertically by adding CPUs

Question 8: Amazon DynamoDB is good for which use case?

1. Structured data, rigid schema
2. Unstructured data, flexible schema

AWS DATABASES ANSWERS

Question 1: Amazon Relational Database Service (RDS) is an example of what type of database?

1. Online transaction processing (OLTP)
2. Online analytics processing (OLAP)
3. No-SQL
4. Data warehouse

Answer: 1

Explanation:

1 is correct. Amazon RDS is an example of a relational database used for online transaction processing (OLTP) workloads. This means its typically used for production databases that process transactions

2 is incorrect. Amazon RDS is not well suited for OLAP workloads

3 is incorrect. Amazon RDS is a relational database, not a No-SQL type of database

4 is incorrect. Amazon RDS is not well suited to be a data warehouse. Amazon RedShift is a better option

Question 2: Which AWS database service offers seamless horizontal scaling?

1. Amazon RDS
2. Amazon RedShift
3. Amazon DynamoDB
4. Database on Amazon EC2

Answer: 3

Explanation:

1 is incorrect. Amazon RDS runs on EC2 instances, so you have to scale vertically by changing instance types

2 is incorrect. Amazon RedShift runs on EC2 instances, so you have to scale vertically by changing instance types

3 is correct. Amazon DynamoDB offers seamless "push-button" horizontal scaling

4 is incorrect. If you run a 3rd party DB on EC2 instances so you have to scale vertically by changing instance types

Question 3: How can fault tolerance be added to an Amazon RDS database?

1. Using read replicas
2. Using multi-AZ
3. Using Global Replicas
4. Using EBS snapshots

Answer: 2

Explanation:

> **1 is incorrect.** Read replicas are used for offloading database reads to improve performance

> **2 is correct.** Multi-AZ creates a standby copy of the master DB in a separate availability zone

> **3 is incorrect.** Global replicas are not a feature of Amazon RDS

> **4 is incorrect.** Snapshots are used to take a point-in-time backup of the database, not for fault tolerance

Question 4: How can an organization enable microsecond latency for a DynamoDB database?

1. Using Amazon ElastiCache
2. Using DynamoDB Auto Scaling
3. Using Read Replicas
4. Using DynamoDB Accelerator (DAX)

Answer: 4

Explanation:

> **1 is incorrect.** Amazon ElastiCache is not typically used in front of DynamoDB

> **2 is incorrect.** This will allow the database to scale but will not achieve microsecond latency

> **3 is incorrect.** Read replicas are used for offloading database reads to improve performance. These are associated with Amazon RDS, not DynamoDB

> **4 is correct.** DynamoDB Accelerator (DAX) is an in-memory cache that increases performance of DynamoDB databases

Question 5: Which AWS database service is a relational, data warehouse?

1. Amazon RedShift
2. Amazon RDS Aurora
3. Amazon DynamoDB
4. Amazon ElastiCache

Answer: 1

Explanation:

> **1 is correct.** RedShift is a relational, SQL database that is well suited for data warehouse use

> **2 is incorrect.** Amazon RDS Aurora is a relational database more suitable to transactional workloads rather than data warehouse workloads

> **3 is incorrect.** Amazon DynamoDB is a No-SQL database used for transactional workloads

> **4 is incorrect.** Amazon ElastiCache is an in-memory cache database

Question 6: Why might an organization decide to move an on-premises database to Amazon RDS?

1. To reduce operational overhead
2. To increase flexibility
3. To eliminate the need to patch management
4. To benefit from seamless scalability

Answer: 1

Explanation:

> **1 is correct.** You can reduce operational overhead by moving to AWS managed services. With RDS this means you no longer need to manage the operating system

> **2 is incorrect.** You do not increase flexibility by moving to Amazon RDS. As it is a managed, hosted service, you will lose some flexibility

> **3 is incorrect.** You do not eliminate the need for patch management on Amazon RDS. Updates are applied during maintenance windows

> **4 is incorrect.** You do not get seamless scalability with RDS. To scale you need to change the instance type which incurs some downtime

Question 7: How do you increase the capacity of an Amazon RDS database?

1. Scaling horizontally, by adding instances
2. Scaling horizontally, by adding RCUs/WCUs
3. Scaling vertically, by changing instance type
4. Scaling vertically by adding CPUs

Answer: 3

Explanation:

> **1 is incorrect.** You do not scale Amazon RDS by adding instances, you must scale RDS vertically

> **2 is incorrect.** You do not add RCUs/WCUs to Amazon RDS - these are used for scaling the capacity of an Amazon DynamoDB database

> **3 is correct.** You can scale Amazon RDS by changing to a larger instance type. This is an example of vertical scaling

> **4 is incorrect.** You need to change instance types to scale RDS, you cannot just add CPUs

Question 8: Amazon DynamoDB is good for which use case?

1. Structured data, rigid schema
2. Unstructured data, flexible schema

Answer: 2

Explanation:

> **1 is incorrect.** Structured data with a rigid schema is a description for a relational SQL type of database such as Amazon RDS

2 is correct. DynamoDB is a No-SQL database which has a flexible schema and is good for unstructured data

AUTO SCALING AND ELASTIC LOAD BALANCING

Auto Scaling and Elastic Load Balancing are features of AWS that you can use separately or together for elasticity and high availability.

AMAZON EC2 AUTO SCALING

Amazon EC2 Auto Scaling automates the process of launching (scaling out) and terminating (scaling in) Amazon EC2 instances based on the traffic demand for your application.

Auto Scaling helps to ensure that you have the correct number of EC2 instances available to handle the application load.

Amazon EC2 Auto Scaling provides elasticity and scalability.

You create collections of EC2 instances, called an Auto Scaling group (ASG).

You can specify the minimum number of instances in each ASG, and AWS Auto Scaling will ensure the group never goes beneath this size.

You can also specify the maximum number of instances in each ASG, and the group will never go above this size.

A desired capacity can be configured, and AWS Auto Scaling will ensure the group has this number of instances.

You can also specify scaling policies that control when Auto Scaling launches or terminates instances.

Scaling policies determine when, if, and how the ASG scales and shrinks (on-demand/dynamic scaling, cyclic/scheduled scaling).

Scaling Plans define the triggers and when instances should be provisioned/de-provisioned.

A launch configuration is the template used to create new EC2 instances and includes parameters such as instance family, instance type, AMI, key pair, and security groups.

AMAZON ELASTIC LOAD BALANCING (ELB)

ELB automatically distributes incoming application traffic across multiple targets, such as Amazon EC2 instances, containers, and IP addresses.

ELB can handle the varying load of your application traffic in a single Availability Zone or across multiple Availability Zones.

ELB features high availability, automatic scaling, and robust security necessary to make your applications fault tolerant.

There are four types of Elastic Load Balancer (ELB) on AWS:

- Application Load Balancer (ALB) – layer 7 load balancer that routes connections based on the content of the request.
- Network Load Balancer (NLB) – layer 4 load balancer that routes connections based on IP protocol data.
- Classic Load Balancer (CLB) – this is the oldest of the three and provides basic load balancing at both layer 4 and layer 7 (not on the exam anymore).
- Gateway Load Balancer (GLB) – distributes connections to virtual appliances and scales them up or down (not on the exam).

APPLICATION LOAD BALANCER (ALB)

ALB is best suited for load balancing of HTTP and HTTPS traffic and provides advanced request routing targeted at the delivery of modern application architectures, including microservices and containers.

Operating at the individual request level (Layer 7), Application Load Balancer routes traffic to targets within Amazon Virtual Private Cloud (Amazon VPC) based on the content of the request.

© 2023 Digital Cloud Training

NETWORK LOAD BALANCER (NLB)

NLB is best suited for load balancing of TCP traffic where extreme performance is required.

Operating at the connection level (Layer 4), Network Load Balancer routes traffic to targets within Amazon Virtual Private Cloud (Amazon VPC) and is capable of handling millions of requests per second while maintaining ultra-low latencies.

Network Load Balancer is also optimized to handle sudden and volatile traffic patterns.

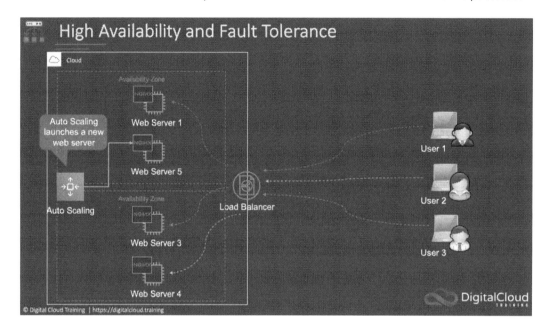

AUTO SCALING AND ELASTIC LOAD BALANCING QUIZ QUESTIONS

Answers and explanations are provided below after the last question in this section.

Question 1: How can a company enable elasticity for an application running on Amazon EC2?

1. By using Amazon EC2 Auto Scaling
2. By using Elastic Load Balancing
3. By configuring multi-AZ
4. By enabling failover in Amazon EC2

Question 2: Which type of Elastic Load Balancer can direct traffic based on the domain name?

1. Classic Load Balancer
2. Network Load Balancer
3. Application Load Balancer
4. Amazon EC2 Load Balancer

Question 3: How does Amazon EC2 Auto Scaling assist with cost-effectiveness?

1. By choosing the most cost-effective instance type
2. By balancing load between instances evenly
3. By launching and terminating instances as demand changes
4. By automating application failover

Question 4: How does Elastic Load Balancing (ELB) assist with fault tolerance?

1. By distributing connections to multiple back-end instances
2. By directing traffic according to latency
3. By caching content closer to users
4. By automatically launching instances

Question 5: Which of the following statements is INCORRECT about Elastic Load Balancing?

1. ELB can distribute connections across availability zones
2. ELB can be Internet facing
3. ELB enables high availability and fault tolerance
4. ELB can distribute connections across regions

Question 6: What does Elastic Load Balancing use to ensure instances are available?

1. EC2 Status Checks
2. CloudWatch Metrics
3. Scaling Plans
4. Health Checks

Question 7: Which type of Elastic Load Balancer routes connections based on IP protocol data at layer 4 only?

1. Classic Load Balancer
2. Network Load Balancer
3. Application Load Balancer

Question 8: What type of template is used by Amazon EC2 Auto Scaling to define instance family, AMI key pair, and security groups?

1. Scaling Plan
2. Launch Configuration
3. Scaling Policy
4. Auto Scaling Group

AUTO SCALING AND ELASTIC LOAD BALANCING ANSWERS

Question 1: How can a company enable elasticity for an application running on Amazon EC2?

1. By using Amazon EC2 Auto Scaling
2. By using Elastic Load Balancing
3. By configuring multi-AZ
4. By enabling failover in Amazon EC2

Answer: 1

Explanation:

1 is correct. Amazon EC2 Auto Scaling enables elasticity for EC2 by launching and terminating instances as demand changes

2 is incorrect. Elastic Load Balancing is used for distributing connections to multiple instances but does not elastically scale the EC2 instances

3 is incorrect. This is not a setting you can configure for EC2

4 is incorrect. Failover may be something you can configure in your application, but it's not something you can configure in Amazon EC2

Question 2: Which type of Elastic Load Balancer can direct traffic based on the domain name?

1. Classic Load Balancer
2. Network Load Balancer
3. Application Load Balancer
4. Amazon EC2 Load Balancer

Answer: 3

Explanation:

1 is incorrect. The classic load balancer cannot do host-based routing

2 is incorrect. The network load balancer cannot do host-based routing

3 is correct. The application load balancer can do host-based routing which means it can direct traffic based on information in the host header such as a domain name

4 is incorrect. This is not a type of Amazon ELB

Question 3: How does Amazon EC2 Auto Scaling assist with cost-effectiveness?

1. By choosing the most cost-effective instance type
2. By balancing load between instances evenly
3. By launching and terminating instances as demand changes
4. By automating application failover

Answer: 3

Explanation:

> **1 is incorrect.** Amazon EC2 Auto Scaling does not choose the most cost-effective instance type for you, you need to choose the instance type to use in the launch configuration

> **2 is incorrect.** This is what Elastic Load Balancing does, and it's not a way of being more cost-effective, it's a way of being more fault-tolerant

> **3 is correct.** Amazon EC2 Auto Scaling launches and terminates instances as demand for your application changes, this ensures you are only paying for instances that you need to service demand

> **4 is incorrect.** Amazon EC2 Auto Scaling does not automate application failover

Question 4: How does Elastic Load Balancing (ELB) assist with fault tolerance?

1. By distributing connections to multiple back-end instances
2. By directing traffic according to latency
3. By caching content closer to users
4. By automatically launching instances

Answer: 1

Explanation:

> **1 is correct.** ELB distributes connections to multiple back-end instances, and this means your application is fault tolerant. You should couple this with Auto Scaling to ensure the right numbers of back-end instances are available

> **2 is incorrect.** ELB does not direct traffic according to latency, and this more about performance than fault tolerance anyway

> **3 is incorrect.** This is not something ELB does. This is more of a performance thing and something Content Delivery Network (CDN) service like Amazon CloudFront does

> **4 is incorrect.** EC2 Auto Scaling is responsible for launching instances, not ELB

Question 5: Which of the following statements is INCORRECT about Elastic Load Balancing?

1. ELB can distribute connections across availability zones
2. ELB can be Internet facing
3. ELB enables high availability and fault tolerance
4. ELB can distribute connections across regions

Answer: 4

Explanation:

> **1 is incorrect.** ELB can handle the varying load of your application traffic in a single Availability Zone or across multiple Availability Zones

> **2 is incorrect.** ELBs can be Internet-facing or internal

> **3 is incorrect.** ELB enables high availability and fault tolerance

> **4 is correct.** ELB cannot distribute connections across regions, only availability zones.

To direct traffic across regions use Amazon Route 53

Question 6: What does Elastic Load Balancing use to ensure instances are available?

1. EC2 Status Checks
2. CloudWatch Metrics
3. Scaling Plans
4. Health Checks

Answer: 4

Explanation:

> **1 is incorrect.** EC2 Status Checks are used by Auto Scaling to check if instances are healthy, but not by ELB

> **2 is incorrect.** ELB does not receive CloudWatch metrics to tell it if an instance is healthy

> **3 is incorrect.** Scaling Plans are used by EC2 Auto Scaling to control how to scale

> **4 is correct.** Health checks are used by ELB to check that an instance is available and healthy

Question 7: Which type of Elastic Load Balancer routes connections based on IP protocol data at layer 4 only?

1. Classic Load Balancer
2. Network Load Balancer
3. Application Load Balancer

Answer: 2

Explanation:

> **1 is incorrect.** The CLB operates at layer 4 and layer 7

> **2 is correct.** The NLB operates at layer 4 of the OSI model only, routing connections based on IP protocol data

> **3 is incorrect.** An ALB operates at layer 7 of the OSI model only, routing connections based on the content of the request

Question 8: What type of template is used by Amazon EC2 Auto Scaling to define instance family, AMI key pair, and security groups?

1. Scaling Plan
2. Launch Configuration
3. Scaling Policy
4. Auto Scaling Group

Answer: 2

Explanation:

> **1 is incorrect.** Scaling Plans define the triggers and when instances should be provisioned/de-provisioned

2 is correct. A launch configuration is the template used to create new EC2 instances and includes parameters such as instance family, instance type, AMI, key pair and security groups

3 is incorrect. Scaling policies determine when, if, and how the ASG scales and shrinks (on-demand/dynamic scaling, cyclic/scheduled scaling)

4 is incorrect. Auto Scaling Group (ASG) are collections of EC2 instances

CONTENT DELIVERY AND DNS SERVICES

This category of AWS services includes services for caching content around the world and providing intelligent Domain Name System (DNS) services for your applications.

AMAZON ROUTE 53

Amazon Route 53 is the AWS Domain Name Service.

Route 53 performs three main functions:

- Domain registration – Route 53 allows you to register domain names.
- Domain Name Service (DNS) – Route 53 translates name to IP addresses using a global network of authoritative DNS servers.
- Health checking – Route 53 sends automated requests to your application to verify that it's reachable, available, and functional.

You can use any combination of these functions.

Route 53 benefits:

- Domain registration.
- DNS service.
- Traffic Flow (send users to the best endpoint).
- Health checking.
- DNS failover (automatically change domain endpoint if system fails).
- Integrates with ELB, S3, and CloudFront as endpoints.

Routing policies determine how Route 53 DNS responds to queries.

The following table highlights the key function of each type of routing policy:

Policy	What it Does
Simple	Simple DNS response providing the IP address associated with a name
Failover	If primary is down (based on health checks), routes to secondary destination
Geolocation	Uses geographic location you're in (e.g. Europe) to route you to the closest region
Geoproximity	Routes you to the closest region within a geographic area
Latency	Directs you based on the lowest latency route to resources
Multivalue answer	Returns several IP addresses and functions as a basic load balancer
Weighted	Uses the relative weights assigned to resources to determine which to route to

AMAZON CLOUDFRONT

Amazon CloudFront is a content delivery network (CDN) that allows you to store (cache) your content at "edge locations" located around the world.

This allows customers to access content more quickly and provides security against DDoS attacks.

CloudFront can be used for data, videos, applications, and APIs.

CloudFront benefits:

*   Cache content at Edge Location for fast distribution to customers.
*   Built-in Distributed Denial of Service (DDoS) attack protection.
*   Integrates with many AWS services (S3, EC2, ELB, Route 53, Lambda).

Origins and Distributions:

*   An origin is the origin of the files that the CDN will distribute.
*   Origins can be either an S3 bucket, an EC2 instance, an Elastic Load Balancer, or Route 53 – can also be external (non-AWS).
*   To distribute content with CloudFront you need to create a distribution.
*   There are two types of distribution: Web Distribution and RTMP Distribution.

CloudFront uses Edge Locations and Regional Edge Caches:

*   An edge location is the location where content is cached (separate to AWS regions/AZs).
*   Requests are automatically routed to the nearest edge location.
*   Regional Edge Caches are located between origin web servers and global edge locations and have a larger cache.
*   Regional Edge caches aim to get content closer to users.

The diagram below shows where Regional Edge Caches and Edge Locations are placed in relation to end users:

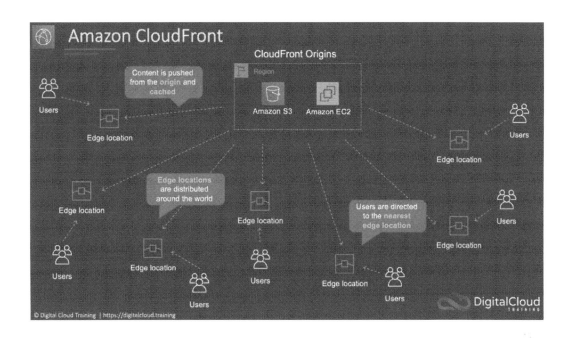

CONTENT DELIVERY AND DNS SERVICES QUIZ QUESTIONS

Answers and explanations are provided below after the last question in this section.

Question 1: Which services does Amazon Route 53 provide?

1. Domain registration, DNS, firewall protection
2. Health checking, DNS, domain registration
3. Health checking, DNS, IP routing
4. Domain registration, DNS, content distribution

Question 2: In Amazon Route 53, what is the name for the configuration item that holds a collection of records belonging to a domain?

1. DNS record
2. Alias
3. Hosted zone
4. Routing Policy

Question 3: How can an organization improve performance for users around the world accessing online videos?

1. Use Amazon Route 53 Failover routing
2. Create an Amazon CloudFront Distribution to host the videos
3. Use Amazon S3 cross-region replication to distribute the media around the world
4. Use Amazon S3 Transfer acceleration to speed up downloads

Question 4: Which services have a Global scope?

1. Amazon CloudFront, Amazon Route 53, Amazon VPC
2. Amazon CloudFront, Amazon Route 53, Amazon CloudWatch
3. AWS Lambda, Amazon CloudFront, Amazon Route 53
4. AWS IAM, Amazon CloudFront, Amazon Route 53

Question 5: Which service has built-in Distributed Denial of Service (DDoS) protection?

1. Amazon Route 53
2. Internet Gateway
3. Amazon CloudFront
4. AWS Direct Connect

Question 6: Which of the following is used to cache data to bring it closer to end users?

1. Amazon CloudFront Edge Location
2. Amazon CloudFront Distribution
3. Amazon CloudFront Origin
4. Amazon CloudFront Bucket

Question 7: Which types of Origin does Amazon CloudFront support?

1. S3 bucket, EC2 instance
2. S3 bucket, RDS database
3. EC2 instance, EFS filesystem
4. EC2 instance, Auto Scaling Group

Question 8: In Amazon Route 53, what is the name for the configuration item that holds a collection of records belonging to a domain?

1. DNS record
2. Alias
3. Hosted zone
4. Routing Policy

CONTENT DELIVERY AND DNS SERVICES ANSWERS

Question 1: Which services does Amazon Route 53 provide?

1. Domain registration, DNS, firewall protection
2. Health checking, DNS, domain registration
3. Health checking, DNS, IP routing
4. Domain registration, DNS, content distribution

Answer: 2

Explanation:

1 is incorrect. Amazon Route 53 does not provide firewall protection

2 is correct. These are the core features of Amazon Route 53

3 is incorrect. Don't confuse routing here with the routing policies in Route 53. Amazon Route 53 is a DNS service that can "route" DNS requests, it does not do IP routing which is a network function

4 is incorrect. Amazon Route 53 does not provide content distribution (CloudFront does)

Question 2: In Amazon Route 53, what is the name for the configuration item that holds a collection of records belonging to a domain?

1. DNS record
2. Alias
3. Hosted zone
4. Routing Policy

Answer: 3

Explanation:

1 is incorrect. A DNS record is an individual record, not a collection of records

2 is incorrect. An Alias is a type of record that points to an AWS resource

3 is correct. A hosted zone represents a set of records belonging to a domain

4 is incorrect. A routing policy determines how Route 53 responds to a query (what records it returns)

Question 3: How can an organization improve performance for users around the world accessing online videos?

1. Use Amazon Route 53 Failover routing
2. Create an Amazon CloudFront Distribution to host the videos
3. Use Amazon S3 cross-region replication to distribute the media around the world
4. Use Amazon S3 Transfer acceleration to speed up downloads

Answer: 2

Explanation:

> **1 is incorrect.** Amazon Route 53 failover routing policy is for failing between active / standby servers. This will not help in this scenario

> **2 is correct.** Amazon CloudFront can be used to get the content cached around the world, closer to users, which will improve performance

> **3 is incorrect.** This is not a good solution. This will get the content closer to users, but you will now have lots of copies of data and need a method of directing traffic to each copy. This is operationally inefficient

> **4 is incorrect.** Amazon S3 Transfer acceleration is used for improving uploads to S3, not downloads

Question 4: Which services have a Global scope?

1. Amazon CloudFront, Amazon Route 53, Amazon VPC
2. Amazon CloudFront, Amazon Route 53, Amazon CloudWatch
3. AWS Lambda, Amazon CloudFront, Amazon Route 53
4. AWS IAM, Amazon CloudFront, Amazon Route 53

Answer: 4

Explanation:

> **1 is incorrect.** Amazon VPC has a regional scope

> **2 is incorrect.** Amazon CloudWatch has a regional scope

> **3 is incorrect.** AWS Lambda has a regional scope

> **4 is correct.** All three of these services have a global scope

Question 5: Which service has built-in Distributed Denial of Service (DDoS) protection?

1. Amazon Route 53
2. Internet Gateway
3. Amazon CloudFront
4. AWS Direct Connect

Answer: 3

Explanation:

> **1 is incorrect.** Amazon Route 53 does not have DDoS protection features

> **2 is incorrect.** An Internet Gateway does not have DDoS protection features

> **3 is correct.** Amazon CloudFront has built-in Distributed Denial of Service (DDoS) attack protection

> **4 is incorrect.** AWS Direct Connect does not have DDoS protection features

Question 6: Which of the following is used to cache data to bring it closer to end users?

1. Amazon CloudFront Edge Location
2. Amazon CloudFront Distribution
3. Amazon CloudFront Origin

4. Amazon CloudFront Bucket

Answer: 1

Explanation:

1 is correct. Edge Locations are part of the AWS Global Infrastructure and are located around the world. They are used to cache content to bring it closer to end users for improved performance

2 is incorrect. A distribution is created within Amazon CloudFront. This is how you configure your origin, settings, and where to cache your file. It is not where the files are cached

3 is incorrect. An origin is the source of the media that needs to be cached around the world

4 is incorrect. A bucket is an Amazon S3 container for holding objects. An S3 bucket can be an origin but it is not where data is cached, it is where it is sourced from

Question 7: Which types of Origin does Amazon CloudFront support?
1. S3 bucket, EC2 instance
2. S3 bucket, RDS database
3. EC2 instance, EFS filesystem
4. EC2 instance, Auto Scaling Group

Answer: 1

Explanation:

1 is correct. You can use S3 buckets and EC2 instances as origins for you CloudFront distribution. You can also use S3 static websites, other HTTP servers using Route 53, instances behind an ELB, and MediaStore Containers

2 is incorrect. You cannot configure an RDS database as an origin

3 is incorrect. You cannot configure an EFS filesystem as an origin

4 is incorrect. You cannot configure an ASG as an origin

Question 8: In Amazon Route 53, what is the name for the configuration item that holds a collection of records belonging to a domain?
1. DNS record
2. Alias
3. Hosted zone
4. Routing Policy

Answer: 3

Explanation:

1 is incorrect. A DNS record is an individual record, not a collection of records

2 is incorrect. An Alias is a type of record that points to an AWS resource

3 is correct. A hosted zone represents a set of records belonging to a domain

4 is incorrect. A routing policy determines how Route 53 responds to a query (what records it returns)

MONITORING AND LOGGING SERVICES

This category of AWS services includes services that provide logging, monitoring, and auditing for your applications running on AWS.

AMAZON CLOUDWATCH

Amazon CloudWatch is a monitoring service for AWS cloud resources and the applications you run on AWS.

CloudWatch is for performance monitoring (CloudTrail is for auditing).

Used to collect and track metrics, collect, and monitor log files, and set alarms.

Automatically react to changes in your AWS resources.

Monitor resources such as:

- EC2 instances.
- DynamoDB tables.
- RDS DB instances.
- Custom metrics generated by applications and services.
- Any log files generated by your applications.

Gain system-wide visibility into resource utilization.

CloudWatch monitoring includes application performance.

Monitor operational health.

CloudWatch is accessed via API, command-line interface, AWS SDKs, and the AWS Management Console.

CloudWatch integrates with IAM.

Amazon CloudWatch Logs lets you monitor and troubleshoot your systems and applications using your existing system, application, and custom log files.

CloudWatch Logs can be used for real time application and system monitoring as well as long term log retention.

CloudWatch Logs keeps logs indefinitely by default.

CloudTrail logs can be sent to CloudWatch Logs for real-time monitoring.

CloudWatch Logs metric filters can evaluate CloudTrail logs for specific terms, phrases, or values.

CloudWatch retains metric data as follows:

- Data points with a period of less than 60 seconds are available for 3 hours. These data points are high-resolution custom metrics.
- Data points with a period of 60 seconds (1 minute) are available for 15 days.
- Data points with a period of 300 seconds (5 minute) are available for 63 days.
- Data points with a period of 3600 seconds (1 hour) are available for 455 days (15 months).

Dashboards allow you to create, customize, interact with, and save graphs of AWS resources and custom metrics.

Alarms can be used to monitor any Amazon CloudWatch metric in your account.

Events are a stream of system events describing changes in your AWS resources.

Logs help you to aggregate, monitor and store logs.

Basic monitoring = 5 mins (free for EC2 Instances, EBS volumes, ELBs and RDS DBs).

Detailed monitoring = 1 min (chargeable).

Metrics are provided automatically for several AWS products and services.

There is no standard metric for memory usage on EC2 instances.

A custom metric is any metric you provide to Amazon CloudWatch (e.g. time to load a web page or application performance).

Options for storing logs:

- CloudWatch Logs.
- Centralized logging system (e.g. Splunk).
- Custom script and store on S3.

Do not store logs on non-persistent disks:

Best practice is to store logs in CloudWatch Logs or S3.

CloudWatch Logs subscription can be used across multiple AWS accounts (using cross account access).

Amazon CloudWatch uses Amazon SNS to send email.

AWS CLOUDTRAIL

AWS CloudTrail is a web service that records activity made on your account and delivers log files to an Amazon S3 bucket.

CloudTrail is for auditing (CloudWatch is for performance monitoring).

CloudTrail is about logging and saves a history of API calls for your AWS account.

Provides visibility into user activity by recording actions taken on your account.

API history enables security analysis, resource change tracking, and compliance auditing.

Logs API calls made via:

- AWS Management Console.
- AWS SDKs.
- Command line tools.
- Higher-level AWS services (such as CloudFormation).

CloudTrail records account activity and service events from most AWS services and logs the following records:

- The identity of the API caller.
- The time of the API call.
- The source IP address of the API caller.
- The request parameters.

- The response elements returned by the AWS service.

CloudTrail is enabled by default.

CloudTrail is per AWS account.

You can consolidate logs from multiple accounts using an S3 bucket:

1. Turn on CloudTrail in the paying account.
2. Create a bucket policy that allows cross-account access.
3. Turn on CloudTrail in the other accounts and use the bucket in the paying account.

You can integrate CloudTrail with CloudWatch Logs to deliver data events captured by CloudTrail to a CloudWatch Logs log stream.

CloudTrail log file integrity validation feature allows you to determine whether a CloudTrail log file was unchanged, deleted, or modified since CloudTrail delivered it to the specified Amazon S3 bucket.

MONITORING AND LOGGING SERVICES QUIZ QUESTIONS

Answers and explanations are provided below after the last question in this section.

Question 1: Which service can be used to record information about API activity in your AWS account?

1. Amazon CloudWatch
2. Amazon CloudTrail

Question 2: Which service can be used for alerting if the CPU is heavily loaded on an EC2 instance?

1. Amazon CloudWatch
2. Amazon CloudTrail

Question 3: Does Amazon CloudTrail permanently record all API activity in your account by default?

1. Yes
2. No

MONITORING AND LOGGING SERVICES ANSWERS

Question 1: Which service can be used to record information about API activity in your AWS account?

1. Amazon CloudWatch
2. Amazon CloudTrail

Answer: 2

Explanation:

> **1 is incorrect.** CloudWatch is used for performance monitoring, not auditing of API activity

> **2 is correct.** CloudTrail can keep a record of all API activity in your account

Question 2: Which service can be used for alerting if the CPU is heavily loaded on an EC2 instance?

1. Amazon CloudWatch
2. Amazon CloudTrail

Answer: 1

Explanation:

> **1 is correct.** CloudWatch is used for performance monitoring

> **2 is incorrect.** CloudTrail is used for auditing, not performance monitoring

Question 3: Does Amazon CloudTrail permanently record all API activity in your account by default?

1. Yes
2. No

Answer: 2

Explanation:

> **1 is incorrect**. By default, Amazon CloudTrail only keeps 90 days of records

> **2 is correct**. By default, Amazon CloudTrail only keeps 90 days of records. To keep records permanently you need to create a Trail and record events to an Amazon S3 bucket

AWS BILLING AND PRICING

AWS Billing and Pricing is one of the key subjects on the AWS Certified Cloud Practitioner exam.

AWS works on a pay as you go model in which you only pay for what you use, when you are using it.

If you turn off resources, you don't pay for them (you may pay for consumed storage).

There are no upfront charges, and you stop paying for a service when you stop using it.

Aside from EC2 reserved instances you are not locked into long term contracts and can terminate whenever you choose to.

Volume discounts are available so the more you use a service the cheaper it gets (per unit used).

There are no termination fees.

The three fundamental drivers of cost with AWS are: compute, storage, and outbound data transfer.

In most cases, there is no charge for inbound data transfer or for data transfer between other AWS services within the same region (there are some exceptions).

Outbound data transfer is aggregated across services and then charged at the outbound data transfer rate.

Free tier allows you to run certain resources for free.

Free tier includes offers that expire after 12 months and offers that never expire.

Pricing policies include:

- Pay as you go.
- Pay less when you reserve.
- Pay even less per unit when using more.
- Pay even less as AWS grows.
- Custom pricing (enterprise customers only).

Free services include:

- Amazon VPC.
- Elastic Beanstalk (but not the resources created).
- CloudFormation (but not the resources created).
- Identity Access Management (IAM).
- Auto Scaling (but not the resources created).
- OpsWorks.
- Consolidated Billing.

Fundamentally charges include:

1. Compute.
2. Storage.

3. Data out.

AMAZON EC2 PRICING

EC2 pricing is based on:

- Clock hours of server uptime.
- Instance configuration.
- Instance type.
- Number of instances.
- Load balancing.
- Detailed monitoring.
- Auto Scaling (resources created).
- Elastic IP addresses (charged if allocated but not used).
- Operating systems and software packages.

There are several pricing models for AWS services, these include:

On Demand:

- Means you pay for compute or database capacity with no long-term commitments of upfront payments.
- You pay for the computer capacity per hour or per second (Linux only, and applies to On-Demand, Reserved and Spot instances).
- Recommended for users who prefer low cost and flexibility without upfront payment or long-term commitments.
- Good for applications with short-term, spiky, or unpredictable workloads that cannot be interrupted.

Dedicated Hosts:

- A dedicated host is an EC2 servers dedicated to a single customer.
- Runs in your VPC.
- Good for when you want to leverage existing server-bound software licenses such as Windows Server, SQL Server, and SUSE Linux Enterprise Server.
- Also good for meeting compliance requirements.

Dedicated Instances:

- Dedicated Instances are Amazon EC2 instances that run in a VPC on hardware that's dedicated to a single customer.
- Dedicated instances are physically isolated at the host hardware level from instances that belong to other AWS accounts.
- Dedicated instances may share hardware with other instances from the same AWS account that are not Dedicated instances.

Spot Instances:

- Purchase spare computing capacity with no upfront commitment at discounted hourly rates.
- Provides up to 90% off the On-Demand price.
- Recommended for applications that have flexible start and end times, applications

that are only feasible at very low compute prices, and users with urgent computing needs for a lot of additional capacity.

- In the old model Spot instances were terminated because of higher competing bids, in the new model this does not happen, but instances still may be terminated (with a 2-minute warning) when EC2 needs the capacity back – note: the exam may not be updated to reflect this yet.

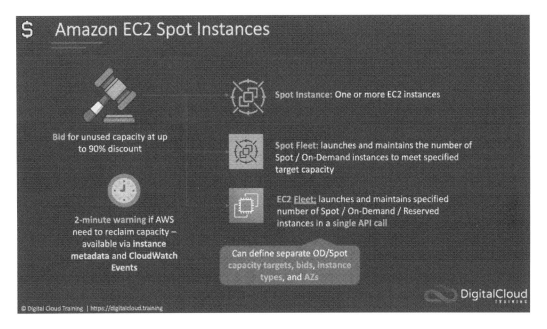

Savings Plans:

- Commitment to a consistent amount of usage (EC2 + Fargate + Lambda); Pay by $/hour; 1 or 3-year commitment.

Reservations:

- Reserved instances provide significant discounts, up to 75% compared to On-Demand pricing, by paying for capacity ahead of time.
- Provide a capacity reservation when applied to a specific Availability Zone.
- Good for applications that have predictable usage, that need reserved capacity, and for customers who can commit to a 1 or 3-year term.

Reservations apply to various services, including:

- Amazon EC2 Reserved Instances.
- Amazon DynamoDB Reserved Capacity.
- Amazon ElastiCache Reserved Nodes.
- Amazon RDS Reserved Instances.
- Amazon RedShift Reserved Instances.

Reservation options include no upfront, partial upfront and all upfront.

Reservation terms are 1 or 3 years.

AMAZON SIMPLE STORAGE SERVICE (S3)

PRICING

Storage pricing is determined by:

- **Storage class** – e.g., Standard or IA.
- **Storage quantity** – data volume stored in your buckets on a per GB basis.
- **Number of requests** – the number and type of requests, e.g., GET, PUT, POST, LIST, COPY.
- **Lifecycle transitions requests** – moving data between storage classes.
- **Data transfer** – data transferred out of an S3 region is charged.

Amazon Glacier pricing

- Extremely low cost and you pay only for what you need with no commitments of upfront fees.
- Charged for requests and data transferred out of Glacier.
- "Amazon Glacier Select" pricing allows queries to run directly on data stored on Glacier without having to retrieve the archive. Priced on amount of data scanned, returned, and number of requests initiated.

AWS SNOWBALL PRICING

Pay a service fee per data transfer job and the cost of shipping the appliance.

Each job allows use of Snowball appliance for 10 days onsite for free.

Data transfer into AWS is free and outbound is charged (per region pricing).

Amazon Relational Database Service (RDS) Pricing

RDS pricing is determined by:

- **Clock hours of server uptime** – amount of time the DB instance is running.
- **Database characteristics** – e.g. database engine, size, and memory class.
- **Database purchase type** – e.g. On-Demand, Reserved.
- **Number of database instances.**
- **Provisioned storage** – backup is included up to 100% of the size of the DB. After the DB is terminated backup storage is charged per GB per month.
- **Additional storage** – the amount of storage in addition to the provisioned storage is charged per GB per month.
- **Requests** – the number of input and output requests to the DB.
- **Deployment type** – single AZ or multi-AZ.
- **Data transfer** – inbound is free, outbound data transfer costs are tiered.
- **Reserved Instances** – RDS RIs can be purchased with No Upfront, Partial Upfront, or All Upfront terms. Available for Aurora, MySQL, MariaDB, Oracle and SQL Server.

AMAZON CLOUDFRONT PRICING

CloudFront pricing is determined by:

- **Traffic distribution** – data transfer and request pricing, varies across regions, and is based on the edge location from which the content is served.

- **Requests** – the number and type of requests (HTTP or HTTPS) and the geographic region in which they are made.
- **Data transfer out** – quantity of data transferred out of CloudFront edge locations.
- There are additional chargeable items such as invalidation requests, field-level encryption requests, and custom SSL certificates.

AWS LAMBDA PRICING

Pay only for what you use and charged based on the number of requests for functions and the time it takes to execute the code.

Price is dependent on the amount of memory allocated to the function.

Amazon Elastic Block Store (EBS) Pricing

Pricing is based on three factors:

- Volumes – volume storage for all EBS volumes type is charged by the amount of GB provisioned per month.
- Snapshots – based on the amount of space consumed by snapshots in S3. Copying snapshots is charged on the amount of data copied across regions.
- Data transfer – inbound data transfer is free, outbound data transfer charges are tiered.

AMAZON DYNAMODB PRICING

Charged based on:

- **Provisioned throughput (write).**
- **Provisioned throughput (read).**
- **Indexed data storage.**
- **Data transfer** – no charge for data transfer between DynamoDB and other AWS services within the same region, across regions is charged on both sides of the transfer.
- **Global tables** – charged based on the resources associated with each replica of the table (replicated write capacity units, or rWCUs).
- **Reserved Capacity** – option available for a one-time upfront fee and commitment to paying a minimum usage level at specific hourly rates for the duration of the term. Additional throughput is charged at standard rates.

On-demand capacity mode:

- Charged for reads and writes
- No need to specify how much capacity is required
- Good for unpredictable workloads

Provisioned capacity mode:

- Specify number of reads and writes per second
- Can use Auto Scaling
- Good for predictable workloads

- Consistent traffic or gradual changes

AWS SUPPORT PLANS

There are four AWS support plans available:

- Basic – billing and account support only (access to forums only).
- Developer – business hours support via email.
- Business – 24×7 email, chat, and phone support.
- Enterprise – 24×7 email, chat, and phone support.

Enterprise support comes with a Technical Account Manager (TAM).

Developer allows one person to open unlimited cases.

Business and Enterprise allow unlimited contacts to open unlimited cases.

	Developer	Business	Enterprise
AWS Trusted Advisor Best Practice Checks	7 Core checks	Full set of checks	Full set of checks
Enhanced Technical Support	• Business hours email access to Cloud Support Associates • Unlimited cases / 1 primary contact	• 24x7 phone, email, and chat access to Cloud Support Engineers • Unlimited cases / unlimited contacts (IAM supported)	• 24x7 phone, email, and chat access to Cloud Support Engineers • Unlimited cases / unlimited contacts (IAM supported)
Case Severity / Response Times*	• General guidance: < 24 hours** • System impaired: < 12 hours**	• General guidance: < 24 hours • System impaired: < 12 hours • Production system impaired: < 4 hours • Production system down: < 1 hour	• General guidance: < 24 hours • System impaired: < 12 hours • Production system impaired: < 4 hours • Production system down: < 1 hour • Business-critical system down: < 15 minutes

	Developer	Business	Enterprise
Architectural Guidance	General	Contextual to your use-cases	Consultative review and guidance based on your applications
Programmatic Case Management		AWS Support API	AWS Support API
Proactive Programs and Services		Access to Infrastructure Event Management for additional fee	• Infrastructure Event Management • Well-Architected Reviews • Access to proactive reviews, workshops, and deep dives
Technical Account Management			Designated Technical Account Manager (TAM) to proactively monitor your environment and assist with optimization and coordinate access to programs and AWS experts
Account Assistance			Concierge Support Team

RESOURCE GROUPS AND TAGGING

Tags are key / value pairs that can be attached to AWS resources.

Tags contain metadata (data about data).

Tags can sometimes be inherited – e.g. resources created by Auto Scaling, CloudFormation or Elastic Beanstalk.

Resource groups make it easy to group resources using the tags that are assigned to them. You can group resources that share one or more tags.

Resource groups contain general information, such as:

- Region.
- Name.
- Health Checks.

And specific information, such as:

- Public & private IP addresses (for EC2).
- Port configurations (for ELB).
- Database engine (for RDS).

AWS ORGANIZATIONS AND CONSOLIDATED BILLING

AWS organizations allows you to consolidate multiple AWS accounts into an organization that you create and centrally manage.

Available in two feature sets:

- Consolidated Billing.
- All features.

Includes root accounts and organizational units.

Policies are applied to root accounts or OUs.

Consolidated billing includes:

- Paying Account – independent and cannot access resources of other accounts.
- Linked Accounts – all linked accounts are independent.

Consolidated billing has the following benefits:

- **One bill** – You get one bill for multiple accounts.
- **Easy tracking** – You can track the charges across multiple accounts and download the combined cost and usage data.
- **Combined usage** – You can combine the usage across all accounts in the organization to share the volume pricing discounts and Reserved Instance discounts. This can result in a lower charge for your project, department, or company than with individual standalone accounts.
- **No extra fee** – Consolidated billing is offered at no additional cost.

Limit of 20 linked accounts (by default).

One bill for multiple AWS accounts.

Easy to track charges and allocate costs.

Volume pricing discounts can be applied to resources.

Billing alerts enabled on the Paying account include data for all Linked accounts (or can be created per Linked account).

Consolidated billing allows you to get volume discounts on all your accounts.

Unused reserved instances (RIs) for EC2 are applied across the group.

CloudTrail is on a per account basis and per region basis but can be aggregated into a single bucket in the paying account.

Best practices:

- Always enable multi-factor authentication (MFA) on the root account.
- Always use a strong and complex password on the root account.
- The Paying account should be used for billing purposes only. Do not deploy resources into the Paying account.

AWS QUICK STARTS

Quick Starts are built by <u>AWS architects</u> and partners to help you deploy popular solutions on AWS, based on AWS best practices for security and high availability.

These reference deployments implement key technologies automatically on the AWS Cloud, often with a single click and in less than an hour.

Leverages CloudFormation.

AWS Cost Calculators and Tools

- **AWS Cost Explorer** – enables you to visualize your usage patterns over time and to identify your underlying cost drivers.
- **AWS Pricing Calculator** – create cost estimates to suit your AWS use cases.

AWS COST EXPLORER

The AWS Cost Explorer is a free tool that allows you to view charts of your costs.

You can view cost data for the past 13 months and forecast how much you are likely to spend over the next three months.

Cost Explorer can be used to discover patterns in how much you spend on AWS resources over time and to identify cost problem areas.

Cost Explorer can help you to identify service usage statistics such as:

- Which services you use the most.
- View metrics for which AZ has the most traffic.
- Which linked account is used the most.

AWS PRICING CALCULATOR

AWS Pricing Calculator is a web-based service that you can use to create cost estimates to suit your AWS use cases.

AWS Pricing Calculator is useful both for people who have never used AWS and for those who want to reorganize or expand their usage.

AWS Pricing Calculator allows you to explore AWS services based on your use cases and create a cost estimate.

AWS COST & USAGE REPORT

Publish AWS billing reports to an Amazon S3 bucket.

Reports break down costs by:

- Hour, day, month, product, product resource, tags.

Can update the report up to three times a day.

Create, retrieve, and delete your reports using the AWS CUR API Reference.

AWS PRICE LIST API

Query the prices of AWS services.

Price List Service API (AKA the Query API) – query with JSON.

AWS Price List API (AKA the Bulk API) – query with HTML.

Alerts via Amazon SNS when prices change.

AWS BUDGETS

Used to track cost, usage, or coverage and utilization for your Reserved Instances and Savings Plans, across multiple dimensions, such as service, or Cost Categories.

Alerting through event-driven alert notifications for when actual or forecasted cost or usage exceeds your budget limit, or when your RI and Savings Plans' coverage or utilization drops below your threshold.

Create annual, quarterly, monthly, or even daily budgets depending on your business needs.

AWS BILLING AND PRICING QUIZ QUESTIONS

Answers and explanations are provided below after the last question in this section.

Question 1: Which pricing model is best suited for a batch computing workload that requires significant compute power and can be stopped at any time?

1. On-demand instances
2. Dedicated instances
3. Spot instances
4. Reserved instances

Question 2: Which AWS services are free?

1. Amazon EC2 Auto Scaling, CloudFormation, IAM
2. Amazon EC2, CloudFormation, IAM
3. Consolidated billing, EC2 Auto Scaling, NAT Gateway
4. IAM, Amazon S3, outbound data transfer

Question 3: With Amazon S3, which of the following are NOT chargeable items?

1. Quantity of data in S3 buckets
2. Lifecycle transitions
3. Transfer Acceleration
4. Inbound data transfer

Question 4: What are the three fundamentals of pricing in AWS?

1. Compute, storage and inbound data transfer
2. Compute, database and Internet connectivity
3. Compute, storage and outbound data transfer
4. Elasticity, agility, and data transfer

Question 5: Which pricing model is highly flexible with no long-term commitments or upfront payments?

1. Dedicated instances
2. Spot instances
3. On-demand
4. Reservations

Question 6: What can you use to assign metadata to AWS resources for cost reporting?

1. Labels
2. Tags
3. ARNs
4. Templates

Question 7: Which AWS pricing feature can be used to take advantage of volume pricing discounts across multiple accounts?

1. Consolidated billing
2. TCO Calculator
3. Enterprise Agreement
4. Cost Explorer

Question 8: Which AWS support plan comes with a Technical Account Manager (TAM)

1. Basic
2. Developer
3. Business
4. Enterprise

Question 9: Which of the following is NOT a payment option for Amazon EC2 reserved instances?

1. No upfront
2. All upfront
3. All at the end
4. Partial upfront

Question 10: Which tool can an IT manager use to forecast costs over the next 3 months?

1. AWS Organizations
2. AWS TCO Calculator
3. AWS Cost Explorer
4. Amazon CloudWatch

AWS BILLING AND PRICING ANSWERS

Question 1: Which pricing model is best suited for a batch computing workload that requires significant compute power and can be stopped at any time?

1. On-demand instances
2. Dedicated instances
3. Spot instances
4. Reserved instances

Answer: 3

Explanation:

> **1 is incorrect.** On-demand would be very expensive for this type of workload
>
> **2 is incorrect.** Dedicated instances are used when you need to run workloads on hardware that's dedicated to a single customer
>
> **3 is correct.** Spot instances are great for this type of workload. You can achieve significant discounts which will mean a big cost saving for such a compute intensive workload. You can be stopped at any time if AWS need the capacity back but that's OK for some batch workloads
>
> **4 is incorrect.** Reserved instances are better for stable long-running workloads where you can commit to a 1 or 3 year term

Question 2: Which AWS services are free?

1. Amazon EC2 Auto Scaling, CloudFormation, IAM
2. Amazon EC2, CloudFormation, IAM
3. Consolidated billing, EC2 Auto Scaling, NAT Gateway
4. IAM, Amazon S3, outbound data transfer

Answer: 1

Explanation:

> **1 is correct.** All these services are free of charge. However, you do pay for resources created by Auto Scaling and CloudFormation
>
> **2 is incorrect.** Amazon EC2 is not free of charge
>
> **3 is incorrect.** NAT Gateways are not free of charge
>
> **4 is incorrect.** Amazon S3 is not free of charge

Question 3: With Amazon S3, which of the following are NOT chargeable items?

1. Quantity of data in S3 buckets
2. Lifecycle transitions
3. Transfer Acceleration
4. Inbound data transfer

Answer: 4

Explanation:

1 is incorrect. This is a chargeable item in Amazon S3

2 is incorrect. This is a chargeable item in Amazon S3

3 is incorrect. This is a chargeable item in Amazon S3

4 is correct. You do not pay for inbound data transfer, only outbound data transfer

Question 4: What are the three fundamentals of pricing in AWS?
1. Compute, storage and inbound data transfer
2. Compute, database and Internet connectivity
3. Compute, storage and outbound data transfer
4. Elasticity, agility, and data transfer

Answer: 3

Explanation:

1 is incorrect. You don't pay for inbound data transfer

2 is incorrect. Internet connectivity is not a fundamental of AWS pricing

3 is correct. Compute, storage and outbound data transfer are the three fundamentals of AWS pricing

4 is incorrect. Elasticity, agility and data transfer are incorrect. These are not fundamentals of AWS pricing. Data transfer is charged but only outbound

Question 5: Which pricing model is highly flexible with no long-term commitments or upfront payments?
1. Dedicated instances
2. Spot instances
3. On-demand
4. Reservations

Answer: 3

Explanation:

1 is incorrect. Dedicated instances are used when you need to run workloads on hardware that's dedicated to a single customer

2 is incorrect. Spot instances are where you purchase spare capacity with no commitments. However, it is less flexible than on-demand as you can't control when capacity will be available

3 is correct. On-demand is the best option when you need the most flexibility. There are no long-term commitments or upfront payments.

4 is incorrect. Reservations are used to get up to 75% discount from the on-demand rate in exchange for a term commitment

Question 6: What can you use to assign metadata to AWS resources for cost reporting?
1. Labels

2. Tags
3. ARNs
4. Templates

Answer: 2

Explanation:

1 is incorrect. Labels are not used for assigning metadata to AWS resources

2 is correct. Tags and resource groups are great tools for assigning metadata to AWS resources and then being able to group resources that share one or more tags

3 is incorrect. ARNs are Amazon Resource Names and are not used for assigning metadata to AWS resources

4 is incorrect. Templates are not used for assigning metadata to AWS resources

Question 7: Which AWS pricing feature can be used to take advantage of volume pricing discounts across multiple accounts?

1. Consolidated billing
2. TCO Calculator
3. Enterprise Agreement
4. Cost Explorer

Answer: 1

Explanation:

1 is correct. With Consolidated billing you can combine the usage across all accounts in the organization to share the volume pricing discounts and Reserved Instance discounts. This can result in a lower charge for your project, department, or company than with individual standalone accounts

2 is incorrect. The TCO calculator is a free tool provided by AWS that allows you to estimate the cost savings of using the AWS Cloud vs. using an on-premise data center

3 is incorrect. This is not an AWS pricing feature

4 is incorrect. The AWS Cost Explorer is a free tool that allows you to view charts of your costs. It is not used for taking advantage of volume pricing discounts across accounts

Question 8: Which AWS support plan comes with a Technical Account Manager (TAM)

1. Basic
2. Developer
3. Business
4. Enterprise

Answer: 4

Explanation:

1 is incorrect. The basic plan does not come with a TAM

2 is incorrect. The developer plan does not come with a TAM

3 is incorrect. The business plan does not come with a TAM

4 is correct. Only the enterprise support plan comes with a TAM

Question 9: Which of the following is NOT a payment option for Amazon EC2 reserved instances?

1. No upfront
2. All upfront
3. All at the end
4. Partial upfront

Answer: 3

Explanation:

1 is incorrect. This is a payment option for Amazon EC2 reserved instances

2 is incorrect. This is a payment option for Amazon EC2 reserved instances

3 is correct. This is not a payment option for Amazon EC2 reserved instances

4 is incorrect. This is a payment option for Amazon EC2 reserved instances

Question 10: Which tool can an IT manager use to forecast costs over the next 3 months?

1. AWS Organizations
2. AWS TCO Calculator
3. AWS Cost Explorer
4. Amazon CloudWatch

Answer: 3

Explanation:

1 is incorrect. AWS organizations allows you to consolidate multiple AWS accounts into an organization that you create and centrally manage

2 is incorrect. The TCO calculator is a free tool provided by AWS that allows you to estimate the cost savings of using the AWS Cloud vs. using an on-premise data center

3 is correct. The AWS Cost Explorer is a free tool that allows you to view charts of your costs. You can view cost data for the past 13 months and forecast how much you are likely to spend over the next three months

4 is incorrect. Amazon CloudWatch is a monitoring tool and cannot be used for forecasting future costs

© 2023 Digital Cloud Training

AWS SECURITY SERVICES

As an AWS customer you inherit all the best practices of AWS policies, architecture, and operational processes.

The AWS Cloud enables a shared responsibility model.

AWS manages security **OF** the cloud; you are responsible for security **IN** the cloud.

You retain control of the security you choose to implement to protect your own content, platform, applications, systems, and networks no differently than you would in an on-site data center.

BENEFITS OF AWS SECURITY

- **Keep Your Data Safe** – the AWS infrastructure puts strong safeguards in place to help.
- **Protect your privacy** – All data is stored in highly secure AWS data centers.
- **Meet Compliance Requirements** – AWS manages dozens of compliance programs in its infrastructure. This means that segments of your compliance have already been completed.
- **Save Money** – cut costs by using AWS data centers. Maintain the highest standard of s security without having to manage your own facility.
- **Scale Quickly** – security scales with your AWS Cloud usage. No matter the size of your business, the AWS infrastructure is designed to keep your data safe.

COMPLIANCE

AWS Cloud Compliance enables you to understand the robust controls in place at AWS to maintain security and data protection in the cloud.

As systems are built on top of AWS Cloud infrastructure, compliance responsibilities will be shared.

Compliance programs include:

- Certifications / attestations.
- Laws, regulations, and privacy.
- Alignments / frameworks.

AWS ARTIFACT

AWS Artifact is your go-to, central resource for compliance-related information that matters to you.

It provides on-demand access to AWS' security and compliance reports and select online agreements.

Reports available in AWS Artifact include our Service Organization Control (SOC) reports, Payment Card Industry (PCI) reports, and certifications from accreditation bodies across geographies and compliance verticals that validate the implementation and operating effectiveness of AWS security controls.

Agreements available in AWS Artifact include the Business Associate Addendum (BAA) and the Nondisclosure Agreement (NDA).

AMAZON GUARDDUTY

Amazon GuardDuty offers threat detection and continuous security monitoring for malicious or unauthorized behavior to help you protect your AWS accounts and workloads.

Intelligent threat detection service.

Detects account compromise, instance compromise, malicious reconnaissance, and bucket compromise.

Continuous monitoring for events across:

- AWS CloudTrail Management Events.
- AWS CloudTrail S3 Data Events.
- Amazon VPC Flow Logs.
- DNS Logs.

AWS WAF & AWS SHIELD

WAF:

- AWS WAF is a web application firewall.
- Protects against common exploits that could compromise application availability, compromise security, or consume excessive resources.
- WAF lets you create rules to filter web traffic based on conditions that include IP addresses, HTTP headers and body, or custom URIs.
- WAF makes it easy to create rules that block common web exploits like SQL injection and cross site scripting.
- The rules are known as Web ACLs.

Shield:

- AWS Shield is a managed Distributed Denial of Service (DDoS) protection service.
- Safeguards web application running on AWS with always-on detection and automatic inline mitigations.
- Helps to minimize application downtime and latency.
- Two tiers – Standard and Advanced.

AWS KEY MANAGEMENT SERVICE (AWS KMS)

AWS Key Management Service gives you centralized control over the encryption keys used to protect your data.

You can create, import, rotate, disable, delete, define usage policies for, and audit the use of encryption keys used to encrypt your data.

AWS Key Management Service is integrated with most other AWS services making it easy to encrypt the data you store in these services with encryption keys you control.

AWS KMS is integrated with AWS CloudTrail which provides you the ability to audit who used which keys, on which resources, and when.

AWS KMS enables developers to easily encrypt data, whether through 1-click encryption in the AWS Management Console or using the AWS SDK to easily add encryption in their application code.

AWS CLOUDHSM

AWS CloudHSM is a cloud-based hardware security module (HSM) that enables you to easily generate and use your own encryption keys on the AWS Cloud.

With CloudHSM, you can manage your own encryption keys using FIPS 140-2 Level 3 validated HSMs.

CloudHSM offers you the flexibility to integrate with your applications using industry-standard APIs, such as PKCS#11, Java Cryptography Extensions (JCE), and Microsoft CryptoNG (CNG) libraries.

AWS CERTIFICATE MANAGER

AWS Certificate Manager is a service that lets you easily provision, manage, and deploy public and private Secure Sockets Layer/Transport Layer Security (SSL/TLS) certificates for use with AWS services and your internal connected resources.

SSL/TLS certificates are used to secure network communications and establish the identity of websites over the Internet as well as resources on private networks.

AWS Certificate Manager removes the time-consuming manual process of purchasing, uploading, and renewing SSL/TLS certificates.

AWS INSPECTOR AND AWS TRUSTED ADVISOR

AWS Inspector:

- Inspector is an automated security assessment service that helps improve the security and compliance of applications deployed on AWS.

- Inspector automatically assesses applications for vulnerabilities or deviations from best practices.
- Uses an agent installed on EC2 instances.
- Instances must be tagged.

AWS Trusted Advisor:

- Trusted Advisor is an online resource that helps to reduce cost, increase performance, and improve security by optimizing your AWS environment.
- Trusted Advisor provides real time guidance to help you provision your resources following best practices.
- Advisor will advise you on Cost Optimization, Performance, Security, and Fault Tolerance.

Trusted Advisor scans your AWS infrastructure and compares is to AWS best practices in five categories:

- Cost Optimization.
- Performance.
- Security.
- Fault Tolerance.
- Service Limits.

Trusted Advisor comes in two versions.

Core Checks and Recommendations (free):

- Access to the 7 core checks to help increase security and performance.
- Checks include S3 bucket permissions, Security Groups, IAM use, MFA on root account, EBS public snapshots, RDS public snapshots.

Full Trusted Advisor Benefits (business and enterprise support plans):

- Full set of checks to help optimize your entire AWS infrastructure.
- Advises on security, performance, cost, fault tolerance and service limits.
- Additional benefits include weekly update notifications, alerts, automated actions with CloudWatch and programmatic access using the AWS Support API.

PENETRATION TESTING

Penetration testing is the practice of testing one's own application's security for vulnerabilities by simulating an attack.

AWS allows penetration testing. There is a limited set of resources on which penetration testing can be performed.

You do not need permission to perform penetration testing against the following services:

- Amazon EC2 instances, NAT Gateways, and Elastic Load Balancers.
- Amazon RDS.
- Amazon CloudFront.
- Amazon Aurora.
- Amazon API Gateways.

- AWS Lambda and Lambda Edge functions.
- Amazon LightSail resources.
- Amazon Elastic Beanstalk environments.

You can read the full vulnerability and penetration testing support policy here.

In case an account is or may be compromised, AWS recommend that the following steps are taken:

1. Change your AWS root account password.
2. Change all IAM user's passwords.
3. Delete or rotate all programmatic (API) access keys.
4. Delete any resources in your account that you did not create.
5. Respond to any notifications you received from AWS through the AWS Support Center and/or contact AWS Support to open a support case.

AWS SINGLE SIGN-ON (AWS SSO)

AWS Single Sign-On is a cloud-based single sign-on (SSO) service that makes it easy to centrally manage SSO access to all your AWS accounts and cloud applications.

It helps you manage SSO access and user permissions across all your AWS accounts in AWS Organizations.

AWS SSO also helps you manage access and permissions to commonly used third-party software as a service (SaaS) applications, AWS SSO-integrated applications as well as custom applications that support Security Assertion Markup Language (SAML) 2.0.

AWS SSO includes a user portal where your end-users can find and access all their assigned AWS accounts, cloud applications, and custom applications in one place.

AMAZON COGNITO

Amazon Cognito lets you add user sign-up, sign-in, and access control to your web and mobile apps quickly and easily.

Amazon Cognito scales to millions of users and supports sign-in with social identity providers, such as Apple, Facebook, Google, and Amazon, and enterprise identity providers via SAML 2.0 and OpenID Connect.

The two main components of AWS Cognito are user pools and identity pools:

- User pools are user directories that provide sign-up and sign-in options for your app users.
- Identity pools enable you to grant your users access to other AWS services.

You can use identity pools and user pools separately or together.

AWS DIRECTORY SERVICES

AWS provides several directory types.

The following three types currently feature on the exam and will be covered on this page:

- Active Directory Service for Microsoft Active Directory.
- Simple AD.
- AD Connector.

As an alternative to the AWS Directory service, you can build your own Microsoft AD DCs in the AWS cloud (on EC2).

The table below summarizes the directory services covered on this page as well as a couple of others, and provides some typical use cases:

Directory Service Option	Description	Use Case
AWS Directory Service for Microsoft Active Directory	AWS-managed full Microsoft AD running on Windows Server 2012 R2	Enterprises that want hosted Microsoft AD or you need LDAP for Linux apps
AD Connector	Allows on-premises users to log into AWS services with their existing AD credentials. Also allows EC2 instances to join AD domain	Single sign-on for on-premises employees and for adding EC2 instances to the domain
Simple AD	Low scale, low cost, AD implementation based on Samba	Simple user directory, or you need LDAP compatibility

AWS SYSTEMS MANAGER PARAMETER STORE

Provides secure, hierarchical storage for configuration data management and secrets management.

It is highly scalable, available, and durable.

You can store data such as passwords, database strings, and license codes as parameter values.

You can store values as plaintext (unencrypted data) or ciphertext (encrypted data).

You can then reference values by using the unique name that you specified when you created the parameter.

AWS SECRETS MANAGER

Like Parameter Store.

Allows native and automatic rotation of keys.

Fine-grained permissions.

Central auditing for secret rotation.

AWS ARTIFACT

AWS Artifact is your go-to, central resource for compliance-related information that matters to you.

It provides on-demand access to AWS' security and compliance reports and select online agreements.

Reports available in AWS Artifact include our Service Organization Control (SOC) reports, Payment Card Industry (PCI) reports, and certifications from accreditation bodies across geographies and compliance verticals that validate the implementation and operating effectiveness of AWS security controls.

Agreements available in AWS Artifact include the Business Associate Addendum (BAA) and the Nondisclosure Agreement (NDA).

AWS SECURITY QUIZ QUESTIONS

Answers and explanations are provided below after the last question in this section.

Question 1: Which tool can be used to find compliance information that relates to the AWS Cloud platform?

1. Amazon Inspector
2. AWS Trusted Advisor
3. AWS Artifact
4. AWS Personal Health Dashboard

Question 2: What is AWS' policy regarding penetration testing?

1. You can only perform penetration testing with permission from AWS
2. You can perform penetration testing against any service and account
3. You can perform penetration testing against selected services without approval
4. Penetration testing is not allowed under any circumstance

Question 3: Which service can assist with protecting against common web-based exploits?

1. AWS Shield
2. AWS Web Application Firewall (WAF)
3. Amazon Route 53
4. AWS CloudHSM

Question 4: Which service is involved with encryption?

1. AWS Key Management Service (KMS)
2. AWS WAF
3. AWS Shield

Question 5: In case of account compromise, which of the following actions should you perform?

1. Delete all IAM users
2. Delete all resources in your account
3. Open a support case with AWS
4. Immediately close your account

AWS SECURITY ANSWERS

Question 1: Which tool can be used to find compliance information that relates to the AWS Cloud platform?

1. Amazon Inspector
2. AWS Trusted Advisor
3. AWS Artifact
4. AWS Personal Health Dashboard

Answer: 3

Explanation:

1 is incorrect. Inspector is an automated security assessment service that helps improve the security and compliance of applications deployed on AWS

2 is incorrect. Trusted Advisor is an online resource that helps to reduce cost, increase performance and improve security by optimizing your AWS environment

3 is correct. AWS Artifact is your go-to, central resource for compliance-related information that matters to you. It provides on-demand access to AWS' security and compliance reports and select online agreements

4 is incorrect. AWS Personal Health Dashboard provides alerts and remediation guidance when AWS is experiencing events that may impact you

Question 2: What is AWS' policy regarding penetration testing?

1. You can only perform penetration testing with permission from AWS
2. You can perform penetration testing against any service and account
3. You can perform penetration testing against selected services without approval
4. Penetration testing is not allowed under any circumstance

Answer: 3

Explanation:

1 is incorrect. This is no longer true; you can now perform penetration testing against selected resources without approval

2 is incorrect. This is not true. You cannot perform penetration testing against all services or against resources in other accounts

3 is correct. This is the new policy. You can now perform penetration testing against several services without approval

4 is incorrect. This is not true. Penetration testing is allowed and there is a policy controlling what you can and can't do

Question 3: Which service can assist with protecting against common web-based exploits?

1. AWS Shield
2. AWS Web Application Firewall (WAF)

3. Amazon Route 53
  4. AWS CloudHSM

Answer: 2

Explanation:

> **1 is incorrect.** AWS Shield is used for preventing DDoS attacks

> **2 is correct.** AWS WAF is a web application firewall that protects against common exploits that could compromise application availability, compromise security or consume excessive resources

> **3 is incorrect.** Amazon Route 53 performs DNS services, health checking services, and domain registration

> **4 is incorrect.** AWS CloudHSM is a cloud-based hardware security module (HSM) that enables you to easily generate and use your own encryption keys on the AWS Cloud

Question 4: Which service is involved with encryption?
  1. AWS Key Management Service (KMS)
  2. AWS WAF
  3. AWS Shield

Answer: 1

Explanation:

> **1 is correct.** AWS KMS is used for managing encryption keys

> **2 is incorrect.** AWS Web Application Firewall protects web applications from common exploits

> **3 is incorrect.** AWS Shield helps protect your resources from DDoS attacks

Question 5: In case of account compromise, which of the following actions should you perform?
  1. Delete all IAM users
  2. Delete all resources in your account
  3. Open a support case with AWS
  4. Immediately close your account

Answer: 3

Explanation:

> **1 is incorrect.** You do not need to delete all IAM users, but you should reset their passwords and delete or rotate API keys

> **2 is incorrect.** You do not need to delete all resources in your account, but you should delete any resources you did not create

> **3 is correct.** You should always respond to any notifications you received from AWS through the AWS Support Center and/or contact AWS Support to open a support case

4 is incorrect. This is unnecessary. You should follow the guidance for how to secure your account

AWS SHARED RESPONSIBILITY MODEL

The AWS shared responsibility model defines what you (as an AWS account holder/user) and AWS are responsible for when it comes to security and compliance.

Security and Compliance is a shared responsibility between AWS and the customer. This shared model can help relieve customer's operational burdens as AWS operates, manages, and controls the components from the host operating system and virtualization layer down to the physical security of the facilities in which the service operates.

The customer assumes responsibility and management of the guest operating system (including updates and security patches), other associated application software as well as the configuration of the AWS provided security group firewall.

AWS are responsible for "Security **of** the Cloud".

- AWS is responsible for protecting the infrastructure that runs all the services offered in the AWS Cloud.
- This infrastructure is composed of the hardware, software, networking, and facilities that run AWS Cloud services.

Customers are responsible for "Security **in** the Cloud".

- For EC2 this includes network level security (NACLs, security groups), operating system patches and updates, IAM user access management, and client and server-side data encryption.

The following diagram shows the split of responsibilities between AWS and the customer:

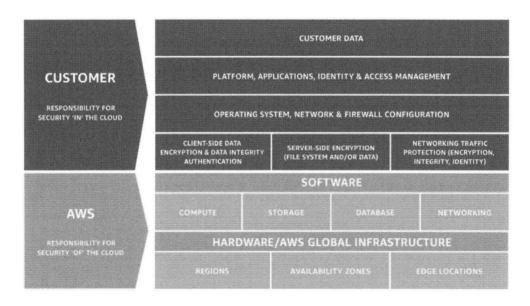

Inherited Controls – Controls which a customer fully inherits from AWS.

- Physical and Environmental controls.

Shared Controls – Controls which apply to both the infrastructure layer and customer layers, but in separate contexts or perspectives.

In the AWS shared security model, a shared control, AWS provides the requirements for the infrastructure and the customer must provide their own control implementation within their use of AWS services.

Examples of shared controls include:

- **Patch Management** – AWS is responsible for patching and fixing flaws within the infrastructure, but customers are responsible for patching their guest OS and applications.
- **Configuration Management** – AWS maintains the configuration of its infrastructure devices, but a customer is responsible for configuring their own guest operating systems, databases, and applications.
- **Awareness & Training** – AWS trains AWS employees, but a customer must train their own employees.

Customer Specific – Controls which are solely the responsibility of the customer based on the application they are deploying within AWS services.

Examples of customer specific controls include:

- Service and Communications Protection or Zone Security which may require a customer to route or zone data within specific security environments.

AWS SHARED RESPONSIBILITY MODEL QUIZ QUESTIONS

Answers and explanations are provided below after the last question in this section.

Question 1: According to the AWS Shared Responsibility model, who is responsible for operating system patching for Amazon EC2 instances?

1. AWS
2. The Customer

Question 2: According to the AWS Shared Responsibility model, who is responsible for configuring server-side encryption for Amazon S3?

1. AWS
2. The Customer

Question 3: According to the AWS Shared Responsibility model, who is responsible for data center security?

1. AWS
2. The customer

Question 4: Which service uses a hardware security module to protect encryption keys in the cloud?

1. AWS Key Management Service (KMS)
2. AWS CloudHSM
3. AWS Service Catalog

Question 5: Which service can be used to find reports on Payment Card Industry (PCI) compliance of the AWS cloud?

1. AWS Service Catalog
2. Amazon Inspector
3. AWS Artifact

Question 6: Who is responsible for patching networking equipment in AWS?

1. AWS
2. The Customer

AWS SHARED RESPONSIBILITY MODEL ANSWERS

Question 1: According to the AWS Shared Responsibility model, who is responsible for operating system patching for Amazon EC2 instances?

1. AWS
2. The Customer

Answer: 2

Explanation:

1 is incorrect. AWS is not responsible for operating system patches on EC2 instances

2 is correct. As a customer, you are responsible for installing patches on the operating systems of your EC2 instances

Question 2: According to the AWS Shared Responsibility model, who is responsible for configuring server-side encryption for Amazon S3?

1. AWS
2. The Customer

Answer: 2

Explanation:

1 is incorrect. AWS are not responsible for configuring server-side encryption. It is up to customers to encrypt their data

2 is correct. AWS are not responsible for configuring server-side encryption. It is up to customers to encrypt their data

Question 3: According to the AWS Shared Responsibility model, who is responsible for data center security?

1. AWS
2. The customer

Answer: 1

Explanation:

1 is correct. AWS is responsible for security "of" the cloud, this includes the facilities in which the services run

2 is incorrect. The customer is not responsible for the data center facilities in which AWS services run

Question 4: Which service uses a hardware security module to protect encryption keys in the cloud?

1. AWS Key Management Service (KMS)
2. AWS CloudHSM
3. AWS Service Catalog

© 2023 Digital Cloud Training

Answer: 2

Explanation:

> **1 is incorrect.** AWS KMS is a shared service and does not use a hardware security module
>
> **2 is correct.** AWS CloudHSM is a cloud-based hardware security module (HSM) that enables you to easily generate and use your own encryption keys on the AWS Cloud
>
> **3 is incorrect.** AWS Service Catalog allows you to centrally manage commonly deployed IT services, and helps you achieve consistent governance to meet your compliance requirements, while enabling users to quickly deploy the approved IT services they need

Question 5: Which service can be used to find reports on Payment Card Industry (PCI) compliance of the AWS cloud?

1. AWS Service Catalog
2. Amazon Inspector
3. AWS Artifact

Answer: 3

Explanation:

> **1 is incorrect.** AWS Service Catalog allows you to centrally manage commonly deployed IT services, and helps you achieve consistent governance to meet your compliance requirements, while enabling users to quickly deploy the approved IT services they need
>
> **2 is incorrect.** Inspector is an automated security assessment service that helps improve the security and compliance of applications deployed on AWS
>
> **3 is correct.** AWS Artifact is your go-to, central resource for compliance-related information that matters to you. It provides on-demand access to AWS' security and compliance reports and select online agreements

Question 6: Who is responsible for patching networking equipment in AWS?

1. AWS
2. The Customer

Answer: 1

Explanation:

> **1 is correct.** AWS are responsible for patching and securing the networking, compute, and storage hardware
>
> **2 is incorrect.** The customer is not responsible for patching hardware

ARCHITECTING FOR THE CLOUD

Architecting for the Cloud is one of the key subjects tested on the Cloud Practitioner exam. This can be dry subject, especially if you're from a non-technical background, but please ensure you're familiar with the concepts at a high-level as questions do come up on the exam.

Please read the following AWS Blog article for additional information:

https://aws.amazon.com/blogs/apn/the-6-pillars-of-the-aws-well-architected-framework/

Cloud computing differs from a traditional environment in the following ways:

IT ASSETS BECOME PROGRAMMABLE RESOURCES

On AWS, servers, databases, storage, and higher-level application components can be instantiated within seconds.

You can treat these as temporary and disposable resources, free from the inflexibility and constraints of a fixed and finite IT infrastructure.

This resets the way you approach change management, testing, reliability, and capacity planning.

GLOBAL, AVAILABLE, AND UNLIMITED CAPACITY

Using the global infrastructure of AWS, you can deploy your application to the AWS Region that best meets your requirements.

For global applications, you can reduce latency to end users around the world by using the Amazon CloudFront content delivery network.

It is also much easier to operate production applications and databases across multiple data centers to achieve high availability and fault tolerance.

HIGHER LEVEL MANAGED SERVICES

AWS customers also have access to a broad set of compute, storage, database, analytics, application, and deployment services.

These services are instantly available to developers and can reduce dependency on in-house specialized skills and allow organizations to deliver new solutions faster.

These services are managed by AWS, which can lower operational complexity and cost.

SECURITY BUILT-IN

The AWS cloud provides governance capabilities that enable continuous monitoring of configuration changes to your IT resources.

Since AWS assets are programmable resources, your security policy can be formalized and embedded with the design of your infrastructure.

DESIGN PRINCIPLES

SCALABILITY

Systems that are expected to grow over time need to be built on top of a scalable architecture.

Scaling Vertically

Scaling vertically takes place through an increase in the specifications of an individual resource (e.g., upgrading a server with a larger hard drive or a faster CPU).

On Amazon EC2, this can easily be achieved by stopping an instance and resizing it to an instance type that has more RAM, CPU, IO, or networking capabilities.

Scaling Horizontally

Scaling horizontally takes place through an increase in the number of resources (e.g., adding more hard drives to a storage array or adding more servers to support an application).

This is a great way to build Internet-scale applications that leverage the elasticity of cloud computing.

The table below provides more information on the differences between horizontal and vertical scaling:

Horizontal Scaling	Vertical Scaling
Add more instances as demand increases	Add more CPU and/or RAM to existing instances as demand increases
No downtime required to scale up or down	Requires a restart to scale up or down
Automatic using services such as AWS Auto-Scaling	Would require scripting or automation tools to automate
Unlimited scalability	Scalability limited by maximum instance size

Stateless applications:

- A stateless application is an application that needs no knowledge of previous interactions and stores no session information.
- A stateless application can scale horizontally since any request can be serviced by any of the available compute resources (e.g., EC2 instances, AWS Lambda functions).

Stateless components:

- Most applications need to maintain state information.
- For example, web applications need to track whether a user is signed in, or else

they might present personalized content based on previous actions.

- Web applications can use HTTP cookies to store information about a session at the client's browser (e.g., items in the shopping cart).
- Consider only storing a unique session identifier in a HTTP cookie and storing more detailed user session information server-side.
- DynamoDB is often used for storing session state to maintain a stateless architecture.
- For larger files a shared storage system can be used such as S3 or EFS.
- SWF can be used for a multi-step workflow.

Stateful components:

- Databases are stateful.
- Many legacy applications are stateful.
- Load balancing with session affinity can be used for horizontal scaling of stateful components.
- Session affinity is however not guaranteed and existing sessions do not benefit from newly launched nodes.

Distributed processing:

- Use cases that involve processing of very large amounts of data (e.g., anything that can't be handled by a single compute resource in a timely manner) require a distributed processing approach.
- By dividing a task and its data into many small fragments of work, you can execute each of them in any of a larger set of available compute resources.

DISPOSABLE RESOURCES INSTEAD OF FIXED SERVERS

Think of servers and other components as temporary resources.

Launch as many as you need and use them only for as long as you need them.

An issue with fixed, long-running servers is that of configuration drift (where change and software patches are applied over time).

This problem can be solved with the "immutable infrastructure" pattern where a server is never updated but instead is replaced with a new one as required.

INSTANTIATING COMPUTE RESOURCES

You don't want to manually set up new resources with their configuration and code.

Use automated, repeatable processes that avoid long lead times and are not prone to human error.

Bootstrapping:

- Execute automated bootstrapping actions to modify default configurations.
- This includes scripts that install software or copy data to bring that resource to a particular state.
- You can parameterize configuration details that vary between different

© 2023 Digital Cloud Training

environments.

Golden Images:

- Some resource types can be launched from a golden image.
- Examples are EC2 instances, RDS instances and EBS volumes.
- A golden image is a snapshot of a particular state for that resource.
- Compared to bootstrapping golden images provide faster start times and remove dependencies to configuration services or third-party repositories.

Infrastructure are Code:

- AWS assets are programmable, so you can apply techniques, practices, and tools from software development to make your whole infrastructure reusable, maintainable, extensible, and testable.

AUTOMATION

In a traditional IT infrastructure, you often must manually react to a variety of events.

When deploying on AWS there is a lot of opportunity for automation.

This improves both your system's stability and the efficiency of your organization.

Examples of automations using AWS services include:

- AWS Elastic Beanstalk – the fastest and simplest way to get an application up and running on AWS.
- Amazon EC2 Auto Recovery – You can create an Amazon CloudWatch alarm that monitors an Amazon EC2 instance and automatically recovers it if it becomes impaired.
- Auto Scaling – With Auto Scaling, you can maintain application availability and scale your Amazon EC2 capacity up or down automatically according to conditions you define.
- Amazon CloudWatch Alarms – You can create a CloudWatch alarm that sends an Amazon Simple Notification Service (Amazon SNS) message when a particular metric goes beyond a specified threshold for a specified number of periods.
- Amazon CloudWatch Events – The CloudWatch service delivers a near real-time stream of system events that describe changes in AWS resources.
- AWS OpsWorks Lifecycle events – AWS OpsWorks supports continuous configuration through lifecycle events that automatically update your instances' configuration to adapt to environment changes.
- AWS Lambda Scheduled events – These events allow you to create a Lambda function and direct AWS Lambda to execute it on a regular schedule.

LOOSE COUPLING

As application complexity increases, a desirable attribute of an IT system is that it can be broken into smaller, loosely coupled components.

This means that IT systems should be designed in a way that reduces interdependencies—a change or a failure in one component should not cascade to other components.

Design principles include:

- **Well-defined interfaces** – reduce interdependencies in a system by enabling interaction only through specific, technology-agnostic interfaces (e.g. RESTful APIs).
- **Service discovery** – disparate resources must have a way of discovering each other without prior knowledge of the network topology.
- **Asynchronous integration** – this is another form of loose coupling where an interaction does not need an immediate response (think SQS queue or Kinesis).
- **Graceful failure** – build applications such that they handle failure in a graceful manner (reduce the impact of failure and implement retries).

SERVICES, NOT SERVERS

With traditional IT infrastructure, organizations must build and operate a wide variety of technology components.

AWS offers a broad set of compute, storage, database, analytics, application, and deployment services that help organizations move faster and lower IT costs.

Managed services:

- On AWS, there is a set of services that provide building blocks that developers can consume to power their applications.
- These managed services include databases, machine learning, analytics, queuing, search, email, notifications, and more.

Serverless architectures:

- Another approach that can reduce the operational complexity of running applications is that of the serverless architectures.
- It is possible to build both event-driven and synchronous services for mobile, web, analytics, and the Internet of Things (IoT) without managing any server infrastructure.

DATABASES

With traditional IT infrastructure, organizations were often limited to the database and storage technologies they could use.

With AWS, these constraints are removed by managed database services that offer enterprise performance at open-source cost.

RELATIONAL DATABASES

Relational databases (often called RDBS or SQL databases) normalize data into well-defined tabular structures known as tables, which consist of rows and columns.

They provide a powerful query language, flexible indexing capabilities, strong integrity controls, and the ability to combine data from multiple tables in a fast and efficient manner.

Amazon RDS is a relational database service.

Scalability:

- Relational databases can scale vertically (e.g. upgrading to a larger RDS DB instance).
- For read-heavy use cases, you can scale horizontally using read replicas.
- For scaling write capacity beyond a single instance data partitioning or sharding is required.

High Availability:

- For production DBs, Amazon recommend the use of RDS Multi-AZ which creates a synchronously replicated standby in another AZ.
- With Multi-AZ RDS can failover to the standby node without administrative intervention.

Anti-Patterns:

- If your application primarily indexes and queries data with no need for joins or complex transactions, consider a NoSQL database instead.
- If you have large binary files (audio, video, and image), it will be more efficient to store the actual files in S3 and only hold the metadata for the files in your database.

NOSQL DATABASES

NoSQL is a term used to describe databases that trade some of the query and transaction capabilities of relational databases for a more flexible data model that seamlessly scales horizontally.

NoSQL databases utilize a variety of data models, including graphs, key-value pairs, and JSON documents.

DynamoDB is Amazon's NoSQL database service.

Scalability:

- NoSQL database engines will typically perform data partitioning and replication to scale both the reads and the writes in a horizontal fashion.

High Availability:

- DynamoDB synchronously replicates data across three facilities in an AWS region for fault tolerance.

Anti-Patterns:

- If your schema cannot be denormalized and your application requires joins or complex transactions, consider a relational database instead.
- If you have large binary files (audio, video, and image), consider storing the files in Amazon S3 and storing the metadata for the files in your database.

DATA WAREHOUSE

A data warehouse is a specialized type of relational database, optimized for analysis and reporting of large amounts of data.

It can be used to combine transactional data from disparate sources making them available for analysis and decision-making.

Amazon Redshift is a managed data warehouse service that is designed to operate at less than a tenth the cost of traditional solutions.

Scalability:

- Amazon Redshift achieves efficient storage and optimum query performance through a combination of massively parallel processing (MPP), columnar data storage, and targeted data compression encoding schemes.
- RedShift is particularly suited to analytic and reporting workloads against very large data sets.

High Availability:

- Redshift has multiple features that enhance the reliability of your data warehouse cluster.
- Multi-node clusters replicate data to other nodes within the cluster.
- Data is continuously backed up to S3.
- RedShift continuously monitors the health of the cluster and re-replicates data from failed drives and replaces nodes as necessary.

Anti-Patterns:

- Because Amazon Redshift is a SQL-based relational database management system (RDBMS), it is compatible with other RDBMS applications and business intelligence tools.
- Although Amazon Redshift provides the functionality of a typical RDBMS, including online transaction processing (OLTP) functions, it is not designed for these workloads.

SEARCH

Applications that require sophisticated search functionality will typically outgrow the capabilities of relational or NoSQL databases.

A search service can be used to index and search both structured and free text format and can support functionality that is not available in other databases, such as customizable result ranking, faceting for filtering, synonyms, stemming, etc.

Scalability:

- Both Amazon CloudSearch and Amazon ES use data partitioning and replication to scale horizontally.

High Availability:

- Both services provide features that store data redundantly across Availability Zones.

REMOVING SINGLE POINTS OF FAILURE

A system is highly available when it can withstand the failure of an individual or multiple components.

Automate recovery and reduce disruption at every layer of your architecture.

INTRODUCING REDUNDANCY

Single points of failure can be removed by introducing redundancy.

In standby redundancy when a resource fails, functionality is recovered on a secondary resource using a process called failover, which typically take some time to complete.

In active redundancy, requests are distributed to multiple redundant compute resources, and when one of them fails, the rest can simply absorb a larger share of the workload.

DETECT FAILURE

Build as much automation as possible in both detecting and reacting to failure.

Services like ELB and Route53 mask failure by routing traffic to healthy endpoint.

Auto Scaling can be configured to automatically replace unhealthy nodes.

You can also replace unhealthy nodes using the EC2 auto- recovery, OpsWorks and Elastic Beanstalk.

DURABLE DATA STORAGE

Design your architecture to protect both data availability and integrity.

Data replication is the technique that introduces redundant copies of data.

It can help horizontally scale read capacity, but it also increases data durability and availability.

Replication can take place in a few different modes:

- Synchronous replication – transactions are acknowledged only after data has been durably stored in both the primary and replica instance. Can be used to protect data integrity (low RPO) and scaling read capacity (with strong consistency).
- Asynchronous replication – changes on the primary node are not immediately reflected on its replicas. Can be used to horizontally scale the system's read capacity (with replication lag), and data durability (with some data loss).
- Quorum-based replication – combines synchronous and asynchronous replication and is good for large-scale distributed database systems.

AUTOMATED MULTI-DATA CENTER RESILIENCE

With traditional infrastructure, failing over between data centers is performed using a disaster recovery plan.

Long distances between data centers mean that latency makes synchronous replication impractical.

Failovers often lead to data loss and costly data recovery processes.

On AWS it is possible to adopt a simpler, more efficient protection from this type of failure.

Each AWS region contains multiple distinct locations called Availability Zones (AZs).

Each AZ is engineered to be isolated from failures in other AZs.

An AZ is a data center, and in some cases, an AZ consists of multiple data centers.

AZs within a region provide inexpensive, low-latency network connectivity to other zones in the same region.

This allows you to replicate your data across data centers in a synchronous manner so that failover can be automated and be transparent for your users.

FAULT ISOLATION AND TRADITIONAL HORIZONTAL SCALING

Though the active redundancy pattern is great for balancing traffic and handling instance or Availability Zone disruptions, it is not sufficient if there is something harmful about the requests themselves.

If a particular request happens to trigger a bug that causes the system to fail over, then the caller may trigger a cascading failure by repeatedly trying the same request against all instances.

One fault-isolating improvement you can make to traditional horizontal scaling is called sharding.

Like the technique traditionally used with data storage systems, instead of spreading traffic from all customers across every node, you can group the instances into shards.

In this way, you can reduce the impact on customers in direct proportion to the number of shards you have.

OPTIMIZE FOR COST

Just by moving existing architectures into the cloud, organizations can reduce capital expenses and drive savings because of the AWS economies of scale.

By iterating and making use of more AWS capabilities there is further opportunity to create cost-optimized cloud architectures.

Right Sizing:

- In some cases, you should select the cheapest type that suits your workload's requirements.
- In other cases, using fewer instances of a larger instance type might result in lower total cost or better performance.
- Benchmark and select the right instance type depending on how your workload utilizes CPU, RAM, network, storage size, and I/O.
- Reduce cost by selecting the right storage solution for your needs.
- E.g. S3 offers a variety of storage classes, including Standard, Reduced Redundancy, and Standard-Infrequent Access.
- EC2, RDS, and ES support different EBS volume types (magnetic, general-purpose SSD, provisioned IOPS SSD) that you should evaluate.

Elasticity:

- Plan to implement Auto Scaling for as many EC2 workloads as possible, so that you horizontally scale up when needed and scale down automatically to reduce cost.
- Automate turning off non-production workloads when not in use.
- Where possible, replace EC2 workloads with AWS managed services that don't require you to take any capacity decisions. For example:
  - ELB.

© 2023 Digital Cloud Training

- o CloudFront.
- o SQS.
- o Kinesis Firehose.
- o Lambda.
- o SES.
- o CloudSearch.
- Or use services for which you can modify capacity as and when need. For example:
  - o DynamoDB.
  - o RDS.
  - o Elasticsearch Service.

Take Advantage of the Variety of Purchasing Options:

- EC2 On-Demand instance pricing gives you maximum flexibility with no long-term commitments.
- There are two more ways to pay for Amazon EC2 instances that can help you reduce spend: Reserved Instances and Spot Instances.

RESERVED CAPACITY

EC2 Reserved Instances allow you to reserve Amazon EC2 computing capacity in exchange for a significantly discounted hourly rate compared to On- Demand instance pricing.

This is ideal for applications with predictable minimum capacity requirements.

SPOT INSTANCES

For less steady workloads, you can consider the use of Spot Instances.

EC2 Spot Instances allow you to bid on spareEC2 computing capacity.

Since Spot Instances are often available at a discount compared to On-Demand pricing, you can significantly reduce the cost of running your applications.

Spot Instances are ideal for workloads that have flexible start and end times.

If the Spot market price increases above your bid price, your instance will be terminated automatically, and you will not be charged for the partial hour that your instance has run.

As a result, Spot Instances are great for workloads that have tolerance to interruption.

CACHING

Caching is a technique that stores previously calculated data for future use.

This technique is used to improve application performance and increase the cost efficiency of an implementation.

It can be applied at multiple layers of an IT architecture.

APPLICATION DATA CACHING

Applications can be designed so that they store and retrieve information from fast, managed, in-memory caches.

Cached information may include the results of I/O-intensive database queries or the outcome of computationally intensive processing.

EDGE CACHING

Copies of static content and dynamic content can be cached at Amazon CloudFront, which is a content delivery network (CDN) consisting of multiple edge locations around the world.

Edge caching allows content to be served by infrastructure that is closer to viewers, lowering latency and giving you the high, sustained data transfer rates needed to deliver large popular objects to end users at scale.

SECURITY

Most of the security tools and techniques that you might already be familiar with in a traditional IT infrastructure can be used in the cloud.

At the same time, AWS allows you to improve your security in a variety of ways.

AWS is a platform that allows you to formalize the design of security controls in the platform itself.

UTILIZE AWS FEATURES FOR DEFENSE IN DEPTH

Network level security includes building a VPC topology that isolates parts of the infrastructure using subnets, security groups, and routing controls.

Services like AWS WAF, a web application firewall, can help protect web applications from SQL injection and other vulnerabilities in application code.

For access control, you can use IAM to define a granular set of policies and assign them to users, groups, and AWS resources.

Finally, the AWS platform offers a breadth of options for protecting data, whether it is in transit or at rest with encryption.

OFFLOAD SECURITY RESPONSIBILITY TO AWS

AWS operates under a shared security responsibility model, where AWS is responsible for the security of the underlying cloud infrastructure, and you are responsible for securing the workloads you deploy in AWS.

REDUCE PRIVILEGED ACCESS

When you treat servers as programmable resources, you can capitalize on that for benefits in the security space as well.

Eliminate the need for guest operating system access to production environments.

If an instance experiences an issue, you can automatically or manually terminate and replace it.

In a traditional environment, service accounts would often be assigned long-term credentials stored in a configuration file.

On AWS, you can instead use IAM roles to grant permissions to applications running on Amazon EC2 instances using short-term credentials.

SECURITY AS CODE

Traditional security frameworks, regulations, and organizational policies define security requirements related to things such as firewall rules, network access controls, internal/external subnets, and operating system hardening.

You can implement these in an AWS environment as well, but you now can capture them all in a script that defines a "Golden Environment."

This means you can create an AWS CloudFormation script that captures your security policy and reliably deploys it.

Security best practices can now be reused among multiple projects and become part of your continuous integration pipeline.

You can perform security testing as part of your release cycle, and automatically discover application gaps and drift from your security policy.

REAL-TIME AUDITING

Testing and auditing your environment is key to moving fast while staying safe.

Traditional approaches that involve periodic checks are not sufficient, especially in agile environments where change is constant.

On AWS, it is possible to implement continuous monitoring and automation of controls to minimize exposure to security risks.

Services like AWS Config, Amazon Inspector, and AWS Trusted Advisor continually monitor for compliance or vulnerabilities.

With AWS Config rules you will also know if some component was out of compliance even for a brief period.

You can implement extensive logging for your applications (using Amazon CloudWatch Logs) and for the actual AWS API calls by enabling AWS CloudTrail.

Logs can then be stored in an immutable manner and automatically processed to either notify or even act on your behalf, protecting your organization from non-compliance.

You can use AWS Lambda, Amazon EMR, the Amazon Elasticsearch Service, or third- party tools from the AWS Marketplace to scan logs to detect things like unused permissions, overuse of privileged accounts, usage of keys, anomalous logins, policy violations, and system abuse.

ARCHITECTING FOR THE CLOUD QUIZ QUESTIONS

Answers and explanations are provided below after the last question in this section.

Question 1: Which architectural benefit of the AWS Cloud assists with lowering operational cost?

1. Higher-level managed services
2. Horizontal scaling
3. Loose coupling
4. Design for failure

Question 2: AWS EC2 Auto Scaling provides which type of scaling?

1. Horizontal
2. Vertical

Question 3: Which type of scaling does an Amazon Read Replica provide?

1. Horizontal
2. Vertical

Question 4: Which of the following is a benefit of API-driven services?

1. You can programmatically and dynamically launch resources
2. You can define services through the AWS management console
3. You get greater fault tolerance
4. Increased reliability

Question 5: Which of the following is an architectural best practice?

1. Design for the future
2. Design monolithic applications
3. Design for failure
4. Use close coupling

Question 6: The best practice "services, not servers" means what?

1. You should try to use more services such as managed services and serverless services
2. You should not use servers such as Amazon EC2
3. Try to only use serverless services

Question 7: How does DynamoDB scale?

1. Vertically
2. Horizontally
3. Both vertically and horizontally

Question 8: Which architectural best practice aims to reduce interdependencies between application components?

1. Automation
2. Services, Not Servers
3. Removing Single Points of Failure
4. Loose Coupling

Question 9: Which of the following is NOT a limitation of scaling vertically?

1. Can reach a limit of maximum instance size
2. Often requires manual intervention
3. Requires a load balancer for distributing load
4. Typically requires downtime

Question 10: Which services can scale horizontally?

1. Amazon DynamoDB, Amazon EC2 Auto Scaling, Amazon S3
2. Amazon DynamoDB, Amazon EFS, Amazon EC2
3. Amazon EC2 Auto Scaling, Amazon S3, NAT Instance

Question 11: If using a well written templates, how can Amazon CloudFormation assist with building secure environments?

1. It does not require privileged access
2. It ensures consistent builds when building repeatably
3. The responsibility is shared with AWS

ARCHITECTING FOR THE CLOUD ANSWERS

Question 1: Which architectural benefit of the AWS Cloud assists with lowering operational cost?

1. Higher-level managed services
2. Horizontal scaling
3. Loose coupling
4. Design for failure

Answer: 1

Explanation:

1 is correct. You can lower operational cost by leveraging managed storage, database, analytics, application and deployment services

2 is incorrect. This does not reduce operational cost; it makes scaling more seamless and typically allows you to scale with less restriction

3 is incorrect. Loose coupling is a best practice for architectures to reduce interdependencies between systems. This does not necessarily lower operational cost, it's more about creating stable applications that have fault tolerance

4 is incorrect. This is a design best practice that asks architects to consider how applications might fail and include mitigations in their design

Question 2: AWS EC2 Auto Scaling provides which type of scaling?

1. Horizontal
2. Vertical

Answer: 1

Explanation:

1 is correct. EC2 Auto Scaling provide horizontal scaling by launching and terminating additional EC2 instances

2 is incorrect. EC2 Auto Scaling does not provide vertical scaling. An example of vertical scaling is changing to a larger instance type

Question 3: Which type of scaling does an Amazon Read Replica provide?

1. Horizontal
2. Vertical

Answer: 1

Explanation:

1 is correct. By offloading reads to another RDS instance you are using horizontal scaling

2 is incorrect. This is not an example of vertical scaling. With vertical scaling you would be changing the RDS instance type

Question 4: Which of the following is a benefit of API-driven services?

1. You can programmatically and dynamically launch resources
2. You can define services through the AWS management console
3. You get greater fault tolerance
4. Increased reliability

Answer: 1

Explanation:

1 is correct. With API driven cloud services, you can programmatically and dynamically launch resources

2 is incorrect. Using the AWS management console is not an example of using the API (though of course it does drive AWS through the API)

3 is incorrect. This is not the case; you don't need API-driven services for fault tolerance

4 is incorrect. This is not the case, API-driven services don't necessarily increase reliability

Question 5: Which of the following is an architectural best practice?

1. Design for the future
2. Design monolithic applications
3. Design for failure
4. Use close coupling

Answer: 3

Explanation:

1 is incorrect. This is not a best practice that AWS discuss, though of course you should plan for growth

2 is incorrect. This is not a best practice. With cloud applications, architects typically prefer microservice architectures without monolithic stacks

3 is correct. This is an architectural best practice. You should always consider what might fail and ensure the application architecture can mitigate the impact of any failure

4 is incorrect. Close coupling is not an architectural best practice. Loose coupling is a best practice that aims to reduce interdependencies between application components

Question 6: The best practice "services, not servers" means what?

1. You should try to use more services such as managed services and serverless services
2. You should not use servers such as Amazon EC2
3. Try to only use serverless services

Answer: 1

Explanation:

1 is correct. This best practice advises customers to leverage more than just Amazon EC2. Try to use the breadth of services available on AWS

2 is incorrect. This is not the message. However, you should try to use the breadth of services available on AWS

3 is incorrect. This would be hard to achieve and is not the advice here. However, you should try to use the breadth of services available on AWS

Question 7: How does DynamoDB scale?

1. Vertically
2. Horizontally
3. Both vertically and horizontally

Answer: 2

Explanation:

1 is incorrect. DynamoDB only scales horizontally

2 is correct. DynamoDB does scale horizontally

3 is incorrect. DynamoDB only scales horizontally

Question 8: Which architectural best practice aims to reduce interdependencies between application components?

1. Automation
2. Services, Not Servers
3. Removing Single Points of Failure
4. Loose Coupling

Answer: 4

Explanation:

1 is incorrect. Automation is not about reducing interdependencies between application components

2 is incorrect. Automation is not about reducing interdependencies between application components

3 is incorrect. Automation is not about reducing interdependencies between application components

4 is correct. Design IT systems to reduce interdependencies. A change or a failure in one component should not cascade to other components

Question 9: Which of the following is NOT a limitation of scaling vertically?

1. Can reach a limit of maximum instance size
2. Often requires manual intervention
3. Requires a load balancer for distributing load
4. Typically requires downtime

Answer: 3

Explanation:

> **1 is incorrect.** This is a valid limitation of scaling vertically
>
> **2 is incorrect.** This is a valid limitation of scaling vertically
>
> **3 is correct.** This is not the case. When scaling EC2 instances horizontally you need a load balancer
>
> **4 is incorrect.** This is a valid limitation of scaling vertically

Question 10: Which services can scale horizontally?

1. Amazon DynamoDB, Amazon EC2 Auto Scaling, Amazon S3
2. Amazon DynamoDB, Amazon EFS, Amazon EC2
3. Amazon EC2 Auto Scaling, Amazon S3, NAT Instance

Answer: 1

Explanation:

> **1 is correct.** All of these services scale horizontally
>
> **2 is incorrect.** Amazon EC2 scales vertically (unless using Auto Scaling)
>
> **3 is incorrect.** A NAT instance runs on Amazon EC2, and you must scale it vertically

Question 11: If using a well written templates, how can Amazon CloudFormation assist with building secure environments?

1. It does not require privileged access
2. It ensures consistent builds when building repeatably
3. The responsibility is shared with AWS

Answer: 2

Explanation:

> **1 is incorrect.** This is not true; you need to have the required privileges to launch each resource
>
> **2 is correct.** When using a well-written template file that secures your resources well, you can then repeatably use the same template to ensure all environments built from the template are secure
>
> **3 is incorrect.** This is not true; you are responsible for resources you launch on AWS

AWS ANALYTICS SERVICES

The are several AWS Analytics services and these include:

- Amazon Athena
- Amazon EMR
- Amazon CloudSearch
- Amazon Elasticsearch Service
- Amazon Kinesis
- Amazon QuickSight
- Amazon Data Pipeline
- AWS Glue
- AWS Lake Formation
- Amazon MSK

In this article we will focus on Athena, EMR, Glue and Kinesis as these are the services that are most likely to come up on the AWS Certified Cloud Practitioner exam. You may also want to follow the links to the other services and read up to understand what they are at a high-level.

AMAZON ELASTIC MAP REDUCE

Amazon EMR is a web service that enables businesses, researchers, data analysts, and developers to easily and cost-effectively process vast amounts of data.

EMR utilizes a hosted Hadoop framework running on Amazon EC2 and Amazon S3.

Managed Hadoop framework for processing huge amounts of data.

Also support Apache Spark, HBase, Presto and Flink.

Most commonly used for log analysis, financial analysis, or extract, translate and loading (ETL) activities.

A Step is a programmatic task for performing some process on the data (e.g. count words).

A cluster is a collection of EC2 instances provisioned by EMR to run your Steps.

EMR uses Apache Hadoop as its distributed data processing engine, which is an open source, Java software framework that supports data-intensive distributed applications running on large clusters of commodity hardware.

EMR is a good place to deploy Apache Spark, an open-source distributed processing used for big data workloads which utilizes in-memory caching and optimized query execution.

You can also launch Presto clusters. Presto is an open-source distributed SQL query engine designed for fast analytic queries against large datasets.

EMR launches all nodes for a given cluster in the same Amazon EC2 Availability Zone.

You can access Amazon EMR by using the AWS Management Console, Command Line Tools, SDKS, or the EMR API.

With EMR you have access to the underlying operating system (you can SSH in).

AMAZON ATHENA

Amazon Athena is an interactive query service that makes it easy to analyze data in Amazon S3 using standard SQL.

Athena is serverless, so there is no infrastructure to manage, and you pay only for the queries that you run.

Athena is easy to use – simply point to your data in Amazon S3, define the schema, and start querying using standard SQL.

Amazon Athena uses Presto with full standard SQL support and works with a variety of standard data formats, including CSV, JSON, ORC, Apache Parquet and Avro.

While Amazon Athena is ideal for quick, ad-hoc querying and integrates with Amazon QuickSight for easy visualization, it can also handle complex analysis, including large joins, window functions, and arrays.

Amazon Athena uses a managed Data Catalog to store information and schemas about the databases and tables that you create for your data stored in Amazon S3.

AWS GLUE

AWS Glue is a fully managed, pay-as-you-go, extract, transform, and load (ETL) service that automates the time-consuming steps of data preparation for analytics.

AWS Glue automatically discovers and profiles data via the Glue Data Catalog, recommends and generates ETL code to transform your source data into target schemas.

AWS Glue runs the ETL jobs on a fully managed, scale-out Apache Spark environment to load your data into its destination.

AWS Glue also allows you to setup, orchestrate, and monitor complex data flows.

You can create and run an ETL job with a few clicks in the AWS Management Console.

Use AWS Glue to discover properties of data, transform it, and prepare it for analytics.

Glue can automatically discover both structured and semi-structured data stored in data lakes on Amazon S3, data warehouses in Amazon Redshift, and various databases running on AWS.

It provides a unified view of data via the Glue Data Catalog that is available for ETL, querying and reporting using services like Amazon Athena, Amazon EMR, and Amazon Redshift Spectrum.

Glue automatically generates Scala or Python code for ETL jobs that you can further customize using tools you are already familiar with.

AWS Glue is serverless, so there are no compute resources to configure and manage.

DATA ANALYSIS AND QUERY USE CASES

Query services like Amazon Athena, data warehouses like Amazon Redshift, and sophisticated data processing frameworks like Amazon EMR, all address different needs and use cases.

Amazon Redshift provides the fastest query performance for enterprise reporting and business intelligence workloads, particularly those involving extremely complex SQL with multiple joins and sub-queries.

Amazon EMR makes it simple and cost effective to run highly distributed processing frameworks such as Hadoop, Spark, and Presto when compared to on-premises deployments. Amazon EMR is flexible – you can run custom applications and code, and define specific compute, memory, storage, and application parameters to optimize your analytic requirements.

Amazon Athena provides the easiest way to run ad-hoc queries for data in S3 without the need to setup or manage any servers.

The table below shows the primary use case and situations for using a few AWS query and analytics services:

AWS Service	Primary Use Case	When to use
Amazon Athena	Query	Run interactive queries against data directly in Amazon S3 without worrying about formatting data or managing infrastructure. Can use with other services such as Amazon RedShift
Amazon RedShift	Data Warehouse	Pull data from many sources, format and organize it, store it, and support complex, high speed queries that produce business reports.
Amazon EMR	Data Processing	Highly distributed processing frameworks such as Hadoop, Spark, and Presto. Run a wide variety of scale-out data processing tasks for applications such as machine learning, graph analytics, data transformation, streaming data.
AWS Glue	ETL Service	Transform and move data to various destinations. Used to prepare and load data for analytics. Data source can be S3, RedShift or another database. Glue Data Catalog can be queried by Athena, EMR and RedShift Spectrum

AMAZON KINESIS

Amazon Kinesis makes it easy to collect, process, and analyze real-time, streaming data so you can get timely insights and react quickly to new information.

Collection of services for processing streams of various data.

Data is processed in "shards".

There are four types of Kinesis service, and these are detailed below.

KINESIS VIDEO STREAMS

Kinesis Video Streams makes it easy to securely stream video from connected devices to AWS for analytics, machine learning (ML), and other processing.

Durably stores, encrypts, and indexes video data streams, and allows access to data through easy-to-use APIs.

Producers provide data streams.

Stores data for 24 hours by default, up to 7 days.

Consumers receive and process data.

Can have multiple shards in a stream.

Supports encryption at rest with server-side encryption (KMS) with a customer master key.

KINESIS DATA STREAMS

Kinesis Data Streams enables you to build custom applications that process or analyze streaming data for specialized needs.

Kinesis Data Streams enables real-time processing of streaming big data.

Kinesis Data Streams is useful for rapidly moving data off data producers and then continuously processing the data.

Kinesis Data Streams **stores data** for later processing by applications (key difference with Firehose which delivers data directly to AWS services).

Common use cases include:

- Accelerated log and data feed intake.
- Real-time metrics and reporting.
- Real-time data analytics.
- Complex stream processing.

KINESIS DATA FIREHOSE

Kinesis Data Firehose is the easiest way to load streaming data into data stores and analytics tools.

Captures, transforms, and loads streaming data.

Enables near real-time analytics with existing business intelligence tools and dashboards.

Kinesis Data Streams can be used as the source(s) to Kinesis Data Firehose.

You can configure Kinesis Data Firehose to transform your data before delivering it.

With Kinesis Data Firehose you don't need to write an application or manage resources.

Firehose can batch, compress, and encrypt data before loading it.

Firehose synchronously replicates data across three AZs as it is transported to destinations.

Each delivery stream stores data records for up to 24 hours.

KINESIS DATA ANALYTICS

Amazon Kinesis Data Analytics is the easiest way to process and analyze real-time, streaming data.

Can use standard SQL queries to process Kinesis data streams.

Provides real-time analysis.

Use cases:

- Generate time-series analytics.
- Feed real-time dashboards.
- Create real-time alerts and notifications.

Quickly author and run powerful SQL code against streaming sources.

Can ingest data from Kinesis Streams and Kinesis Firehose.

Output to S3, RedShift, Elasticsearch and Kinesis Data Streams.

Sits over Kinesis Data Streams and Kinesis Data Firehose.

AWS ANALYTICS SERVICES QUIZ QUESTIONS

Answers and explanations are provided below after the last question in this section.

Question 1: Which service can be used to analyze data on Amazon S3 using serverless SQL queries?

1. Amazon Kinesis
2. Amazon Athena
3. AWS Glue
4. AWS Lambda

Question 2: A company has many manufacturing facilities with sensors that send environmental information. Which service can ingest and process the data?

1. Amazon Kinesis
2. AWS Glue
3. AWS Data Pipeline

Question 3: A company needs an interactive dashboard for business intelligence. What should they use?

1. Amazon CloudWatch
2. AWS CloudTrail
3. Amazon QuickSight

AWS ANALYTICS SERVICES ANSWERS

Question 1: Which service can be used to analyze data on Amazon S3 using serverless SQL queries?

1. Amazon Kinesis
2. Amazon Athena
3. AWS Glue
4. AWS Lambda

Answer: 2

Explanation:

1 is incorrect. Kinesis processes real-time streaming data

2 is correct. Athena is a serverless service that allows you to directly analyze data in Amazon S3 using SQL queries

3 is incorrect. AWS Glue is an extract, transform and load (ETL) service. It is not used for running SQL queries

4 is incorrect. AWS Lambda is a serverless, function computing service

Question 2: A company has many manufacturing facilities with sensors that send environmental information. Which service can ingest and process the data?

1. Amazon Kinesis
2. AWS Glue
3. AWS Data Pipeline

Answer: 1

Explanation:

1 is correct. Amazon Kinesis makes it easy to collect, process, and analyze real-time, streaming data. It is ideal for this use case

2 is incorrect. AWS Glue is a fully managed extract, transform, and load (ETL) service is used to prepare and load data for analytics

3 is incorrect. AWS Data Pipeline is a web service that helps you reliably process and move data between different AWS compute and storage services, as well as on-premises data sources, at specified intervals

Question 3: A company needs an interactive dashboard for business intelligence. What should they use?

1. Amazon CloudWatch
2. AWS CloudTrail
3. Amazon QuickSight

Answer: 3

Explanation:

1 is incorrect. CloudWatch is a monitoring service for performance monitoring

2 is incorrect. CloudTrail is an auditing service used for monitoring API activity.

3 is correct. Amazon QuickSight is a fast, cloud-powered business intelligence service that makes it easy to deliver insights to everyone in your organization

APPLICATION INTEGRATION SERVICES

The AWS application integration services are a family of services that enable decoupled communication between applications.

These services provide decoupling for microservices, distributed systems, and serverless applications.

AWS application integration services allow you to connect apps, without needing to write custom code to enable interoperability.

Decoupled applications can interoperate whilst being resilient to the failure or overload of any individual component.

The following services are involved with application integration:

Service	What it does	Example use cases
Simple Queue Service (SQS)	Messaging queue; store and forward patterns	Building distributed / decoupled applications
Simple Notification Service (SNS)	Set up, operate, and send notifications from the cloud	Send email notification when CloudWatch alarm is triggered
Step Functions	Out-of-the-box coordination of AWS service components with visual workflow	Order processing workflow
Simple Workflow Service (SWF)	Need to support external processes or specialized execution logic	Human-enabled workflows like an order fulfilment system or for procedural requests
Amazon MQ	Message broker service for Apache Active MQ and RabbitMQ	Need a message queue that supports industry standard APIs and protocols; migrate queues to AWS

AMAZON SIMPLE NOTIFICATION SERVICE

Amazon Simple Notification Service (Amazon SNS) is a web service that makes it easy to set up, operate, and send notifications from the cloud.

Amazon SNS is used for building and integrating loosely-coupled, distributed applications.

SNS provides instantaneous, push-based delivery (no polling).

SNS concepts:

- Topics – how you label and group different endpoints that you send messages to.
- Subscriptions – the endpoints that a topic sends messages to.
- Publishers – the person/alarm/event that gives SNS the message that needs to be sent.

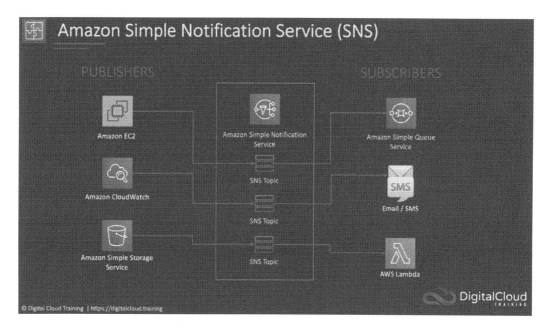

Amazon Simple Notification Service (SNS)

SNS usage:

- Send automated or manual notifications.
- Send notification to email, mobile (SMS), SQS, and HTTP endpoints.
- Closely integrated with other AWS services such as CloudWatch so that alarms, events, and actions in your AWS account can trigger notifications.

Uses simple APIs and easy integration with applications.

Flexible message delivery is provided over multiple transport protocols.

Offered under an inexpensive, pay-as-you-go model with no up-front costs.

The web-based AWS Management Console offers the simplicity of a point-and-click interface.

Data type is JSON.

SNS supports a wide variety of needs including event notification, monitoring applications, workflow systems, time-sensitive information updates, mobile applications, and any other application that generates or consumes notifications.

SNS Subscribers:

- HTTP.
- HTTPS.
- Email.
- Email-JSON.
- SQS.
- Application.
- Lambda.

SNS supports notifications over multiple transport protocols:

- HTTP/HTTPS – subscribers specify a URL as part of the subscription registration.

- Email/Email-JSON – messages are sent to registered addresses as email (text-based or JSON-object).
- SQS – users can specify an SQS standard queue as the endpoint.
- SMS – messages are sent to registered phone numbers as SMS text messages.

Topic names are limited to 256 characters.

SNS supports CloudTrail auditing for authenticated calls.

SNS provides durable storage of all messages that it receives (across multiple AZs).

AMAZON SIMPLE QUEUE SERVICE (AMAZON SQS)

Amazon Simple Queue Service (SQS) is a distributed queue system.

Amazon SQS enables you to send, store, and receive messages between software components.

An Amazon SQS queue is a temporary repository for messages that are awaiting processing.

The SQS queue acts as a buffer between the component producing and saving data, and the component receiving the data for processing.

This is known as decoupling / loose coupling and helps to enable elasticity for your application.

Amazon SQS is pull-based, not push-based (like Amazon SNS).

AMAZON SIMPLE WORKFLOW SERVICE (AMAZON SWF)

Amazon Simple Workflow Service (SWF) is a web service that makes it easy to coordinate work across distributed application components.

Amazon SWF is used for processing background jobs that have parallel or sequential steps.

You can think of Amazon SWF as a fully managed state tracker and task coordinator.

Use Amazon SWF if your app's steps take more than 500 milliseconds to complete, you need to track the state of processing, or you need to recover or retry if a task fails.

With SWF you can create distributed asynchronous systems as workflows.

Tracks the state of your workflow which you interact and update via API.

Best suited for human-enabled workflows like an order fulfilment system or for procedural requests.

AWS recommends that for new applications customers consider AWS Step Functions instead of SWF.

AMAZON MQ

Amazon MQ is a managed message broker service for ActiveMQ.

Amazon MQ supports industry-standard APIs and protocols so you can migrate messaging and applications without rewriting code.

Amazon MQ provides cost-efficient and flexible messaging capacity.

Amazon MQ manages the administration and maintenance of ActiveMQ brokers and automatically provisions infrastructure for high availability.

AWS STEP FUNCTIONS

AWS Step Functions can be used to coordinate the components of distributed applications as a series of steps in a visual workflow.

You can quickly build and run state machines to execute the steps of your application in a reliable and scalable fashion.

How it works:

1. Define the steps of your workflow in the JSON-based Amazon States Language. The visual console automatically graphs each step in the order of execution.

2. Start an execution to visualize and verify the steps of your application are operating as intended. The console highlights the real-time status of each step and provides a detailed history of every execution.

3. AWS Step Functions operates and scales the steps of your application and underlying compute for you to help ensure your application executes reliably under increasing demand.

It is a managed workflow and orchestration platform.

APPLICATION INTEGRATION SERVICES QUIZ QUESTIONS

Answers and explanations are provided below after the last question in this section.

Question 1: An application needs to send SMS text messages to customers to notify them of product updates. Which service can be used?

1. AWS Step Functions
2. Amazon Simple Queue Service
3. Amazon Simple Notification Service
4. AWS Lambda

Question 2: A company needs to orchestrate several batch processes on AWS. Which serverless service can assist?

1. Amazon Simple Workflow Service
2. Amazon Simple Queue Service
3. Amazon EventBridge
4. AWS Step Functions

Question 3: How can a company decouple an application which uses a message-oriented API to communicate data between application components?

1. Create an Amazon SQS queue
2. Create an Amazon SNS topic
3. Create an AWS Step Functions state machine
4. Create an Amazon VPC route table

Question 4: How can an application be configured to send a notification to multiple Amazon SQS queues?

1. Use a FIFO queue
2. Use an Amazon SNS topic
3. Create an AWS Step Functions state machine

APPLICATION INTEGRATION SERVICES ANSWERS

Question 1: An application needs to send SMS text messages to customers to notify them of product updates. Which service can be used?

1. AWS Step Functions
2. Amazon Simple Queue Service
3. Amazon Simple Notification Service
4. AWS Lambda

Answer: 3

Explanation:

1 is incorrect. Step Functions is a workflow orchestration service

2 is incorrect. SQS is a message bus, it does not send SMS text messages

3 is correct. SNS is a notification service that uses a publisher/subscriber model. It can be used to send notifications over multiple transport protocols including SMS text message

4 is incorrect. Lambda is a compute service that runs serverless functions

Question 2: A company needs to orchestrate several batch processes on AWS. Which serverless service can assist?

1. Amazon Simple Workflow Service
2. Amazon Simple Queue Service
3. Amazon EventBridge
4. AWS Step Functions

Answer: 4

Explanation:

1 is incorrect. SWF is not a serverless service

2 is incorrect. SQS is a message queue, not an orchestration service

3 is incorrect. Watch out for distractors you don't recognize! This is a service we haven't covered and it's an event bus, not an orchestration service

4 is correct. Step Functions is a workflow orchestration service and is serverless

Question 3: How can a company decouple an application which uses a message-oriented API to communicate data between application components?

1. Create an Amazon SQS queue
2. Create an Amazon SNS topic
3. Create an AWS Step Functions state machine
4. Create an Amazon VPC route table

Answer: 1

Explanation:

1 is correct. An Amazon Simple Queue Service queue can be used to decouple application components

2 is incorrect. An SNS topic can be used to decouple applications. However, it is not used with messages, it is used with notifications

3 is incorrect. A Step Functions state machine cannot be used to decouple an application using a message-oriented API

4 is incorrect. An Amazon VPC route table controls routing in a VPC, it has nothing to do with decoupling applications

Question 4: How can an application be configured to send a notification to multiple Amazon SQS queues?

1. Use a FIFO queue
2. Use an Amazon SNS topic
3. Create an AWS Step Functions state machine

Answer: 2

Explanation:

1 is incorrect. It doesn't matter which type of queue you use in this case

2 is correct. Multiple SQS queues can be subscribed to a single SNS topic

3 is incorrect. A state machine does not need to be used, an SNS topic is a better solution

AWS CLOUD MANAGEMENT

The AWS Cloud Management services can be used for account management, configuration compliance, application delivery, and systems management.

AWS ORGANIZATIONS

AWS organizations allows you to consolidate multiple AWS accounts into an organization that you create and centrally manage.

Available in two feature sets:

- Consolidated Billing.
- All features.

Includes root accounts and organizational units.

Policies are applied to root accounts or OUs.

Consolidated billing includes:

- Paying Account – independent and cannot access resources of other accounts.
- Linked Accounts – all linked accounts are independent.

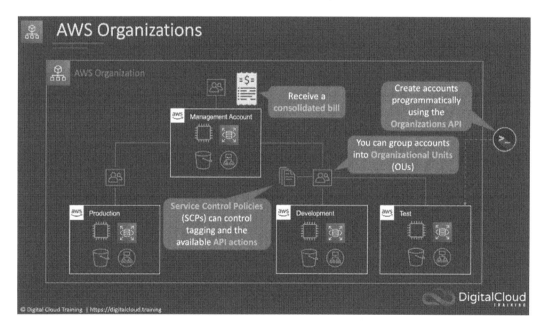

AWS CONTROL TOWER

Simplifies the process of creating multi-account environments.

Sets up governance, compliance, and security guardrails for you.

Integrates with other services and features to setup the environment for you including:

- AWS Organizations, SCPs, OUs, AWS Config, AWS CloudTrail, Amazon S3, Amazon SNS, AWS CloudFormation, AWS Service Catalog, AWS Single Sign-On (SSO).

Examples of guardrails AWS Control Tower can configure for you include:

- Disallowing public write access to Amazon Simple Storage Service (Amazon S3) buckets.
- Disallowing access as a root user without multi-factor authentication.
- Enabling encryption for Amazon EBS volumes attached to Amazon EC2 instances.

AWS Config

AWS Config is a fully managed service that provides you with an AWS resource inventory, configuration history, and configuration change notifications to enable security and regulatory compliance.

With AWS Config, you can discover existing and deleted AWS resources, determine your overall compliance against rules, and dive into configuration details of a resource at any point in time. AWS Config enables compliance auditing, security analysis, resource change tracking, and troubleshooting.

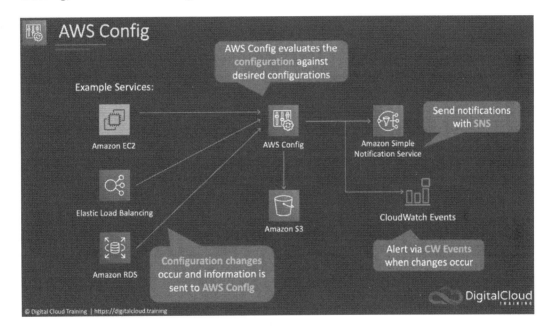

AWS SERVICE CATALOG

AWS Service Catalog allows organizations to create and manage catalogs of IT services that are approved for use on AWS.

AWS Service Catalog allows you to centrally manage commonly deployed IT services.

IT services can include virtual machine images, servers, software, and databases and multi-tier application architectures.

Enables users to quickly deploy only the approved IT services they need.

AWS SYSTEMS MANAGER

Manages many AWS resources including Amazon EC2, Amazon S3, Amazon RDS etc.

Systems Manager Components:

- Automation.
- Run Command.
- Inventory.
- Patch Manager.
- Session Manager.
- Parameter Store.

AWS PERSONAL HEALTH DASHBOARD

AWS Personal Health Dashboard provides alerts and remediation guidance when AWS is experiencing events that may impact you.

Personal Health Dashboard gives you a personalized view into the performance and availability of the AWS services underlying your AWS resources.

The dashboard displays relevant and timely information to help you manage events in progress.

Also provides proactive notification to help you plan for scheduled activities.

Alerts are triggered by changes in the health of AWS resources, giving you event visibility, and guidance to help quickly diagnose and resolve issues.

You get a personalized view of the status of the AWS services that power your applications, enabling you to quickly see when AWS is experiencing issues that may impact you.

Also provides forward looking notifications, and you can set up alerts across multiple channels, including email and mobile notifications, so you receive timely and relevant information to help plan for scheduled changes that may affect you.

Alerts include remediation details and specific guidance to enable you to take immediate action to address AWS events impacting your resources.

Can integrate with Amazon CloudWatch Events, enabling you to build custom rules and select targets such as AWS Lambda functions to define automated remediation actions.

The AWS Health API allows you to integrate health data and notifications with your existing in-house or third-party IT Management tools.

SERVICE HEALTH DASHBOARD

AWS publishes up-to-the-minute information on service availability.

This information is not personalized to you (unlike Personal Health Dashboard).

AWS OPSWORKS

AWS OpsWorks is a configuration management service that provides managed instances of Chef and Puppet.

Updates include patching, updating, backup, configuration, and compliance management.

AWS TRUSTED ADVISOR

AWS Trusted Advisor is an online tool that provides you real time guidance to help you provision your resources following AWS best practices.

Trusted Advisor checks help optimize your AWS infrastructure, improve security and performance, reduce your overall costs, and monitor service limits.

AWS Basic Support and AWS Developer Support customers get access to 6 security checks (S3 Bucket Permissions, Security Groups – Specific Ports Unrestricted, IAM Use, MFA on Root Account, EBS Public Snapshots, RDS Public Snapshots) and 50 service limit checks.

AWS Business Support and AWS Enterprise Support customers get access to all 115 Trusted Advisor checks (14 cost optimization, 17 security, 24 fault tolerance, 10 performance, and 50 service limits) and recommendations.

AWS CLOUDFORMATION

AWS CloudFormation provides a common language for you to describe and provision all the infrastructure resources in your cloud environment.

CloudFormation allows you to use a simple text file to model and provision, in an automated and secure manner, all the resources needed for your applications across all regions and accounts.

This file serves as the single source of truth for your cloud environment.

You can use JSON or YAML to describe what AWS resources you want to create and configure.

AWS CLOUD MANAGEMENT QUIZ QUESTIONS

Answers and explanations are provided below after the last question in this section.

Question 1: An organization is looking for a way to deploy infrastructure on AWS in different regions whilst ensuring consistent configuration. Which service should the organization use?

1. AWS Elastic Beanstalk
2. AWS Config
3. AWS CloudFormation
4. AWS Launch Configuration

Question 2: Which service uses JSON or YAML template files to deploy infrastructure as code?

1. AWS CloudFormation
2. AWS Elastic Beanstalk

Question 3: Which service can be used to automatically create an Amazon VPC and then launch an EC2 instance, Auto Scaling Group and Elastic Load balancer?

1. AWS Elastic Beanstalk
2. AWS Management Console
3. AWS API
4. AWS CloudFormation

Question 4: AWS Trusted advisor does NOT provide advice on which of the following?

1. Cost optimization
2. Performance
3. Total Cost of Ownership (TCO)
4. Security
5. Fault Tolerance

Question 5: A company wishes to determine if there will be any AWS maintenance that could affect their systems over the next few days. Which service should they check?

1. AWS Service Health Dashboard
2. AWS Personal Health Dashboard
3. AWS Trusted Advisor

Question 6: A company wishes to restrict the applications users can launch to an approved list. Which service should they use?

1. AWS Service Catalog
2. AWS Systems Manager
3. AWS OpsWorks

Question 7: AWS Systems Manager includes management of all the following

components, except:

1. Automation
2. Patch Manager
3. Session Manager
4. Service Catalog

AWS CLOUD MANAGEMENT ANSWERS

Question 1: An organization is looking for a way to deploy infrastructure on AWS in different regions whilst ensuring consistent configuration. Which service should the organization use?

1. AWS Elastic Beanstalk
2. AWS Config
3. AWS CloudFormation
4. AWS Launch Configuration

Answer: 3

Explanation:

> **1 is incorrect.** Elastic Beanstalk is used for automating the build and management of web applications, not infrastructure. It is more limited in scope compared to CloudFormation

> **2 is incorrect.** AWS Config is a service that enables you to assess, audit, and evaluate the configurations of your AWS resources

> **3 is correct.** CloudFormation can be used to deploy infrastructure as code using pre-written template files in JSON or YAML.

> **4 is incorrect.** A launch configuration is associated with EC2 Auto Scaling and is used to define the instance family, type, AMI and security groups for instances launched using the ASG

Question 2: Which service uses JSON or YAML template files to deploy infrastructure as code?

1. AWS CloudFormation
2. AWS Elastic Beanstalk

Answer: 1

Explanation:

> **1 is correct.** AWS CloudFormation deploys infrastructure using code and uses JSON or YAML template files

> **2 is incorrect.** Elastic Beanstalk deploys applications on EC2 (PaaS), and uses ZIP or WAR files (or Git) to upload the code

Question 3: Which service can be used to automatically create an Amazon VPC and then launch an EC2 instance, Auto Scaling Group and Elastic Load balancer?

1. AWS Elastic Beanstalk
2. AWS Management Console
3. AWS API
4. AWS CloudFormation

Answer: 4

Explanation:

1 is incorrect. Elastic Beanstalk cannot be used to create a VPC

2 is incorrect. You can do all this manually using the AWS Management Console but not automatically

3 is incorrect. The AWS API is used to launch services, but it is not an automation tool. You need an automation tool that can use the AWS API to launch services

4 is correct. AWS CloudFormation can automate the entire process of creating a VPC and launching many different types of resources into it

Question 4: AWS Trusted advisor does NOT provide advice on which of the following?

1. Cost optimization
2. Performance
3. Total Cost of Ownership (TCO)
4. Security
5. Fault Tolerance

Answer: 3

Explanation:

1 is incorrect. AWS Trusted advisor does provide advice on cost optimization

2 is incorrect. AWS Trusted advisor does provide advice on performance

3 is correct. AWS Trusted advisor does not provide advice on TCO

4 is incorrect. AWS Trusted advisor does provide advice on security

4 is incorrect. AWS Trusted advisor does provide advice on fault tolerance

Question 5: A company wishes to determine if there will be any AWS maintenance that could affect their systems over the next few days. Which service should they check?

1. AWS Service Health Dashboard
2. AWS Personal Health Dashboard
3. AWS Trusted Advisor

Answer: 2

Explanation:

1 is incorrect. The service health dashboard only shows what's happening now and is not personalized

2 is correct. The personal health dashboard provides a personalized view of events that could affect your systems

3 is incorrect. Trusted Advisor helps you to build your systems according to best practice

Question 6: A company wishes to restrict the applications users can launch to an approved list. Which service should they use?

1. AWS Service Catalog

2. AWS Systems Manager
3. AWS OpsWorks

Answer: 1

Explanation:

1 is correct. This service can be used to provide an approved catalog of services and applications that users can launch

2 is incorrect. Systems Manager does not provide a catalog of approved services

3 is incorrect. OpsWorks does not provide a catalog of approved services

Question 7: AWS Systems Manager includes management of all the following components, except:

1. Automation
2. Patch Manager
3. Session Manager
4. Service Catalog

Answer: 4

Explanation:

1 is incorrect. Automation IS a component of Systems Manager.

2 is incorrect. Patch Manager IS a component of Systems Manager and enables users to deploy operating system and software applications automatically across lots of instances.

3 is incorrect. Session Manager IS a component of Systems Manager and enables users to manage their EC2 instances at scale without having to log into your servers.

4 is correct. Service Catalog is NOT a component of Systems Manager and is its own standalone service enabling users to create and manage catalogs of IT services that are approved for use on AWS.

AWS MACHINE LEARNING SERVICES

This article discusses AWS Machine Learning Services in the context of the AWS Certified Cloud Practitioner Exam. Services in this category come up regularly in questions and are usually high level.

AWS REKOGNITION

Add image and video analysis to your applications.

Identify objects, people, text, scenes, and activities in images and videos.

Processes videos stored in an Amazon S3 bucket.

Publish completion status to Amazon SNS Topic.

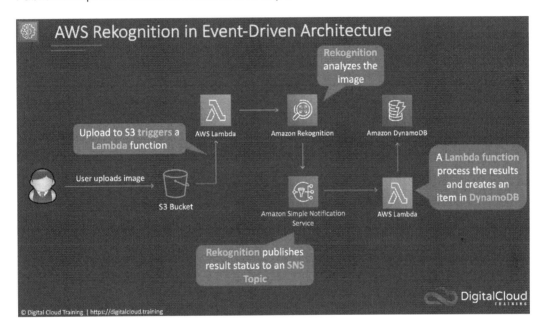

AMAZON TRANSCRIBE

Add speech to text capabilities to applications.

Recorded speech can be converted to text before it can be used in applications.

Uses a deep learning process called automatic speech recognition (ASR) to convert speech to text quickly and accurately.

AMAZON TRANSLATE

Neural machine translation service that delivers fast, high-quality, and affordable language translation.

Uses deep learning models to deliver more accurate and more natural sounding translation.

Localize content such as websites and applications for your diverse users.

AMAZON TEXTRACT

Automatically extract printed text, handwriting, and data from any document.

Features:

- Optical character recognition (OCR).
- Identifies relationships, structure, and text.
- Uses AI to extract text and structured data.
- Recognizes handwriting as well as printed text.
- Can extract from documents such as PDFs, images, forms, and tables.
- Understands context. For example, know what data to extract from a receipt or invoice.

AMAZON SAGEMAKER

Helps data scientists and developers to prepare, build, train, and deploy high-quality machine learning (ML) models.

ML development activities including:

- Data preparation.
- Feature engineering.
- Statistical bias detection.
- Auto-ML.
- Training and tuning.
- Hosting.
- Monitoring.
- Workflows.

AMAZON COMPREHEND

Natural-language processing (NLP) service.

Uses machine learning to uncover information in unstructured data.

Can identify critical elements in data, including references to language, people, and places, and the text files can be categorized by relevant topics.

In real time, you can automatically and accurately detect customer sentiment in your content.

AMAZON LEX

Conversational AI for Chatbots.

Build conversational interfaces into any application using voice and text.

Build bots to increase contact center productivity, automate simple tasks, and drive operational efficiencies across the enterprise.

AMAZON POLLY

Turns text into lifelike speech.

Create applications that talk and build entirely new categories of speech-enabled products.

Text-to-Speech (TTS) service uses advanced deep learning technologies to synthesize natural sounding human speech.

AMAZON FORECAST

Time-series forecasting service.

Uses ML and is built for business metrics analysis.

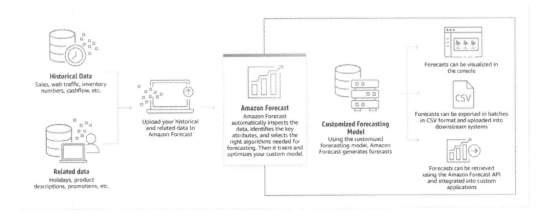

AMAZON DEVOPS GURU

Cloud operations service for improving application operational performance and availability.

Detect behaviors that deviate from normal operating patterns.

Benefits:

- Automatically detect operational issues.
- Resolve issues with ML-powered insights.
- Elastically scale operational analytics.
- Uses ML to reduce alarm noise.

AWS MACHINE LEARNING SERVICES QUIZ QUESTIONS

Answers and explanations are provided below after the last question in this section.

Question 1: A company recorded some support call conversations in mp4 files. How can the company extract the audio into a text document?

1. Use Amazon Translate
2. Use Amazon Polly
3. Use Amazon Transcribe

Question 2: An application is being built that needs to identify faces in images. Which service can be used?

1. AWS Polly
2. AWS Lambda
3. AWS Rekognition

AWS MACHINE LEARNING SERVICES ANSWERS

Question 1: A company recorded some support call conversations in mp4 files. How can the company extract the audio into a text document?

1. Use Amazon Translate
2. Use Amazon Polly
3. Use Amazon Transcribe

Answer: 3

Explanation:

> **1 is incorrect.** Translate is used to translate text between different languages
>
> **2 is incorrect.** Polly turns text into speech
>
> **3 is correct.** Transcribe can extract audio to text

Question 2: An application is being built that needs to identify faces in images. Which service can be used?

1. AWS Polly
2. AWS Lambda
3. AWS Rekognition

Answer: 3

Explanation:

> **1 is incorrect.** Polly is used to turn text into speech
>
> **2 is incorrect.** Lambda can be used for a variety of jobs if you write the code. However, it's not the best service for this use case
>
> **3 is correct.** Rekognition can be used to detect faces in images

ADDITIONAL AWS SERVICES

There are Additional AWS Services & Tools that may feature on the exam. Often you do not need to know these at a deep level but do need to understand what they are and what they are used for.

On this page, you'll find some high-level details and links for more information on some of these services and tools.

Exam tip: *Before sitting the exam, it would be wise to go through the AWS console and pick out any services you're not familiar with and do a bit of reading up on them using the AWS documentation.*

Note: *If a service starts appearing regularly on the exam it may be moved to the main cheat sheet for the AWS service category.*

COMPUTE

AMAZON ELASTIC CONTAINER SERVICE FOR KUBERNETES (EKS)

- Amazon Elastic Container Service for Kubernetes (EKS) is a managed Kubernetes service that makes it easy for you to run Kubernetes on AWS without needing to install, operate, and maintain your own Kubernetes control plane.
- EKS is certified Kubernetes conformant, so existing applications running on upstream Kubernetes are compatible with Amazon EKS.
- EKS automatically manages the availability and scalability of the Kubernetes control plane nodes that are responsible for starting and stopping containers, scheduling containers on virtual machines, storing cluster data, and other tasks.
- EKS automatically detects and replaces unhealthy control plane nodes for each cluster.
- Generally available but only in limited regions currently.
- https://aws.amazon.com/eks/features/

DATABASE

AMAZON NEPTUNE

- Amazon Neptune is a fast, reliable, fully managed graph database service that makes it easy to build and run applications that work with highly connected datasets.
- With Amazon Neptune, you can create sophisticated, interactive graph applications that can query billions of relationships in milliseconds.
- SQL queries for highly connected data are complex and hard to tune for performance. Instead, Amazon Neptune allows you to use the popular graph query languages Apache TinkerPop Gremlin and W3C's SPARQL to execute powerful queries that are easy to write and perform well on connected data.

- https://aws.amazon.com/neptune/features/

MIGRATION

AWS MIGRATION HUB

- AWS Migration Hub provides a single location to track the progress of application migrations across multiple AWS and partner solutions.
- Using Migration Hub allows you to choose the AWS and partner migration tools that best fit your needs, while providing visibility into the status of migrations across your portfolio of applications.
- For example, you might use AWS Database Migration Service, AWS Server Migration Service, and partner migration tools such as ATADATA ATAmotion, CloudEndure Live Migration, or RiverMeadow Server Migration SaaS to migrate an application comprised of a database, virtualized web servers, and a bare metal server.
- Using Migration Hub, you can view the migration progress of all the resources in the application.
- https://aws.amazon.com/migration-hub/features/

AWS DATABASE MIGRATION SERVICE

- AWS Database Migration Service helps you migrate databases to AWS quickly and securely.
- The source database remains fully operational during the migration, minimizing downtime to applications that rely on the database.
- The AWS Database Migration Service can migrate your data to and from most widely used commercial and open-source databases.
- AWS Database Migration Service supports homogenous migrations such as Oracle to Oracle, as well as heterogeneous migrations between different database platforms, such as Oracle or Microsoft SQL Server to Amazon Aurora.
- With AWS Database Migration Service, you can continuously replicate your data with high availability and consolidate databases into a petabyte-scale data warehouse by streaming data to Amazon Redshift and Amazon S3.
- https://aws.amazon.com/dms/

AWS SERVER MIGRATION SERVICE

- AWS Server Migration Service (SMS) is an agentless service which makes it easier and faster for you to migrate thousands of on-premises workloads to AWS
- AWS SMS allows you to automate, schedule, and track incremental replications of live server volumes, making it easier for you to coordinate large-scale server migrations
- https://aws.amazon.com/server-migration-service/

NETWORKING & CONTENT DELIVERY

AMAZON API GATEWAY

- Amazon API Gateway is a fully managed service that makes it easy for developers to create, publish, maintain, monitor, and secure APIs at any scale.
- With a few clicks in the AWS Management Console, you can create an API that acts as a "front door" for applications to access data, business logic, or functionality from your back-end services.
- Back-end services may include Amazon Elastic Compute Cloud (Amazon EC2), code running on AWS Lambda, or any web application.
- https://aws.amazon.com/api-gateway/features/

DEVELOPER TOOLS

AWS CODESTAR

- AWS CodeStar enables you to quickly develop, build, and deploy applications on AWS. AWS CodeStar provides a unified user interface, enabling you to easily manage your software development activities in one place.
- With AWS CodeStar, you can set up your entire continuous delivery toolchain in minutes, allowing you to start releasing code faster. AWS CodeStar makes it easy for your whole team to work together securely, allowing you to easily manage access and add owners, contributors, and viewers to your projects.
- With AWS CodeStar, you can use a variety of project templates to start developing applications on Amazon EC2, AWS Lambda, and AWS Elastic Beanstalk.
- AWS CodeStar projects support many popular programming languages including Java, JavaScript, PHP, Ruby, and Python.
- https://aws.amazon.com/codestar/features/

AWS CODECOMMIT

- AWS CodeCommit is a fully managed source control service that hosts secure Git-based repositories.
- It makes it easy for teams to collaborate on code in a secure and highly scalable ecosystem.
- CodeCommit eliminates the need to operate your own source control system or worry about scaling its infrastructure.
- You can use CodeCommit to securely store anything from source code to binaries, and it works seamlessly with your existing Git tools.
- https://aws.amazon.com/codecommit/features/

AWS CODEBUILD

- AWS CodeBuild is a fully managed continuous integration service that compiles source code, runs tests, and produces software packages that are ready to deploy.
- With CodeBuild, you don't need to provision, manage, and scale your own build servers. CodeBuild scales continuously and processes multiple builds concurrently,

so your builds are not left waiting in a queue.
- You can get started quickly by using prepackaged build environments, or you can create custom build environments that use your own build tools.
- With CodeBuild, you are charged by the minute for the compute resources you use.
- https://aws.amazon.com/codebuild/features/

AWS CODEDEPLOY

- AWS CodeDeploy is a fully managed deployment service that automates software deployments to a variety of computer services such as Amazon EC2, AWS Lambda, and your on-premises servers.
- AWS CodeDeploy makes it easier for you to rapidly release new features, helps you avoid downtime during application deployment, and handles the complexity of updating your applications.
- You can use AWS CodeDeploy to automate software deployments, eliminating the need for error-prone manual operations. The service scales to match your deployment needs, from a single Lambda function to thousands of EC2 instances.
- https://aws.amazon.com/codedeploy/features/

AWS CODEPIPELINE

- AWS CodePipeline is a fully managed continuous delivery service that helps you automate your release pipelines for fast and reliable application and infrastructure updates.
- CodePipeline automates the build, test, and deploy phases of your release process every time there is a code change, based on the release model you define.
- This enables you to deliver features and updates rapidly and reliably.
- You can easily integrate AWS CodePipeline with third-party services such as GitHub or with your own custom plugin.
- https://aws.amazon.com/codepipeline/features/

AWS X-RAY

- AWS X-Ray helps developers analyze and debug production, distributed applications, such as those built using a microservices architecture.
- With X-Ray, you can understand how your application and its underlying services are performing to identify and troubleshoot the root cause of performance issues and errors.
- X-Ray provides an end-to-end view of requests as they travel through your application and shows a map of your application's underlying components.
- You can use X-Ray to analyze both applications in development and in production, from simple three-tier applications to complex microservices applications consisting of thousands of services.
- https://aws.amazon.com/xray/features/
- https://aws.amazon.com/servicecatalog/features/

AWS MANAGED SERVICES

- AWS Managed Services provides ongoing management of your AWS infrastructure so you can focus on your applications.
- By implementing best practices to maintain your infrastructure, AWS Managed Services helps to reduce your operational overhead and risk.
- AWS Managed Services automates common activities such as change requests, monitoring, patch management, security, and backup services, and provides full-lifecycle services to provision, run, and support your infrastructure.
- AWS Managed Services delivers consistent operations management and predictable results by following ITIL® best practices, and provides tooling and automation to increase efficiency, and reduce your operational overhead and risk.
- https://aws.amazon.com/managed-services/#

ANALYTICS

AMAZON ATHENA

- Amazon Athena is an interactive query service that makes it easy to analyze data in Amazon S3 using standard SQL.
- Athena is serverless, so there is no infrastructure to manage, and you pay only for the queries that you run.
- With a few clicks in the AWS Management Console, customers can point Athena at their data stored in S3 and begin using standard SQL to run ad-hoc queries and get results in seconds.
- You can use Athena to process logs, perform ad-hoc analysis, and run interactive queries
- Athena scales automatically – executing queries in parallel – so results are fast, even with large datasets and complex queries.
- https://aws.amazon.com/athena/features/

AMAZON EMR

- Amazon Elastic Map Reduce (EMR) provides a managed Hadoop framework that makes it easy, fast, and cost-effective to process vast amounts of data across dynamically scalable Amazon EC2 instances.
- You can also run other popular distributed frameworks such as Apache Spark, HBase, Presto, and Flink in Amazon EMR, and interact with data in other AWS data stores such as Amazon S3 and Amazon DynamoDB.
- Amazon EMR securely and reliably handles a broad set of big data use cases, including log analysis, web indexing, data transformations (ETL), machine learning, financial analysis, scientific simulation, and bioinformatic.
- https://aws.amazon.com/emr/features/

AMAZON CLOUDSEARCH

- Amazon CloudSearch is a managed service in the AWS Cloud that makes it simple and cost-effective to set up, manage, and scale a search solution for your website

- or application.
- Amazon CloudSearch supports 34 languages and popular search features such as highlighting, autocomplete, and geospatial search.
- https://aws.amazon.com/cloudsearch/

AMAZON ELASTICSEARCH

- Amazon Elasticsearch Service is a fully managed service that makes it easy for you to deploy, secure, operate, and scale Elasticsearch to search, analyze, and visualize data in real-time.
- With Amazon Elasticsearch Service you get easy-to-use APIs and real-time analytics capabilities to power use-cases such as log analytics, full-text search, application monitoring, and clickstream analytics, with enterprise-grade availability, scalability, and security.
- https://aws.amazon.com/elasticsearch-service/features/

AMAZON KINESIS

- Amazon Kinesis makes it easy to collect, process, and analyze real-time, streaming data so you can get timely insights and react quickly to new information.
- There are four types of Kinesis service:
  - Kinesis Video Streams makes it easy to securely stream video from connected devices to AWS for analytics, machine learning (ML), and other processing.
  - Kinesis Data Streams enables you to build custom applications that process or analyze streaming data for specialized needs.
  - Kinesis Data Firehose is the easiest way to load streaming data into data stores and analytics tools.
  - Amazon Kinesis Data Analytics is the easiest way to process and analyze real-time, streaming data.
- https://aws.amazon.com/kinesis/
- https://digitalcloud.training/certification-training/aws-solutions-architect-associate/analytics/amazon-kinesis/

AWS DATA PIPELINE

- AWS Data Pipeline is a web service that helps you reliably process and move data between different AWS compute and storage services, as well as on-premises data sources, at specified intervals.
- With AWS Data Pipeline, you can regularly access your data where it's stored, transform, and process it at scale, and efficiently transfer the results to AWS services such as Amazon S3, Amazon RDS, Amazon DynamoDB, and Amazon EMR.
- AWS Data Pipeline helps you easily create complex data processing workloads that are fault tolerant, repeatable, and highly available.
- https://aws.amazon.com/datapipeline/

AWS GLUE

- AWS Glue is a fully managed extract, transform, and load (ETL) service that makes

it easy for customers to prepare and load their data for analytics.
- You can create and run an ETL job with a few clicks in the AWS Management Console.
- You simply point AWS Glue to your data stored on AWS, and AWS Glue discovers your data and stores the associated metadata (e.g. table definition and schema) in the AWS Glue Data Catalog.
- Once cataloged, your data is immediately searchable, queryable, and available for ETL.
- AWS Glue generates the code to execute your data transformations and data loading processes.
- https://aws.amazon.com/glue/features/

MEDIA SERVICES

AMAZON ELASTIC TRANSCODER

- Amazon Elastic Transcoder is media transcoding in the cloud.
- It is designed to be a highly scalable, easy to use and a cost-effective way for developers and businesses to convert (or "transcode") media files from their source format into versions that will playback on devices like smartphones, tablets, and PCs.
- https://aws.amazon.com/elastictranscoder/

MOBILE SERVICES

AWS APPSYNC

- AWS AppSync makes it easy to build data-driven mobile and browser-based apps that deliver responsive, collaborative experiences by keeping the data updated when devices are connected, enabling the app to use local data when offline, and synchronizing the data when the devices reconnect.
- AWS AppSync uses the open standard GraphQL query language so you can request, change, and subscribe to the exact data you need with just a few lines of code.
- https://aws.amazon.com/appsync/product-details/

AWS DEVICE FARM

- AWS Device Farm is an app testing service that lets you test and interact with your Android, iOS, and web apps on many devices at once, or reproduce issues on a device in real time.
- View video, screenshots, logs, and performance data to pinpoint and fix issues and increase quality before shipping your app.
- https://aws.amazon.com/device-farm/

END USER COMPUTING

AMAZON WORKSPACES

- Amazon WorkSpaces is a managed, secure cloud desktop service. You can use Amazon WorkSpaces to provision either Windows or Linux desktops in just a few minutes and quickly scale to provide thousands of desktops to workers across the globe.
- Amazon WorkSpaces offers you an easy way to provide a secure, managed, cloud-based virtual desktop experience to your end-users.
- Unlike traditional on-premises Virtual Desktop Infrastructure (VDI) solutions, you don't have to worry about procuring, deploying, and managing a complex environment – Amazon WorkSpaces takes care of the heavy lifting and provides a fully managed service.
- https://aws.amazon.com/workspaces/features/

AWS APPSTREAM

- Fully managed non-persistent application streaming service.
- Alternative to popular products such as Citrix XenApp.
- https://aws.amazon.com/appstream2/features/

AWS WORKLINK

- Provides secure, one-click access to your internal websites and web apps using mobile phone browsers.
- Does not require VPN client or App.
- https://aws.amazon.com/worklink/features/

AWS WORKDOCS

- Fully managed, secure content creation, storage, and collaboration service
- Create, edit, and share content that's centrally stored on AWS.
- https://aws.amazon.com/workdocs/features/

INTERNET OF THINGS (IOT)

AWS IOT CORE

- Describes the network of physical objects that are embedded with sensors or software.
- Each IoT device can communicate and exchange data with other devices and systems.
- Use cases include:
    - Smart home automation.
    - Smart healthcare.
    - Manufacturing.
    - Agriculture.

- Allows you to connect IoT devices to the AWS cloud without the need to provision or manage servers.
- Can support billions of devices and trillions of messages.
- https://aws.amazon.com/iot-core/features/

ADDITIONAL AWS SERVICES QUIZ QUESTIONS

Answers and explanations are provided below after the last question in this section.

Question 1: A company moves data between Amazon S3, RDS and EMR. Which service can help to process and move data between services?

1. Amazon Athena
2. Amazon QuickSight
3. AWS Data Pipeline

Question 2: Which service can be used to migrate an on-premises database to Amazon RDS?

1. AWS Server Migration Service
2. AWS Transfer for SMTP
3. Application Discovery Service
4. Database Migration Service

Question 3: Which service can be used to migrate exabytes of data into the AWS Cloud?

1. AWS Snowmobile
2. AWS Snowball

Question 4: Which service can be used to migrate 50TB of data quickly and affordably to Amazon S3 for a company with a slow Internet connection?

1. Amazon S3 Transfer Acceleration
2. Amazon S3 multi-part upload
3. AWS Snowball
4. AWS Snowmobile

Question 5: How can a company migrate a database from Amazon EC2 to RDS without downtime?

1. Create an RDS read replica and then promote replica to master
2. Create a new database from an EBS snapshot
3. Migrate using the AWS Database Migration Service (DMS)

Question 6: A company needs to migrate several TB of data from an on-premises NAS device to Amazon FSx. Which service can the company use to migrate the data over a VPN connection?

1. AWS Database Migration Service (DMS)
2. AWS Snowball Edge
3. AWS DataSync
4. Amazon S3 Transfer Acceleration

ADDITIONAL AWS SERVICES ANSWERS

Question 1: A company moves data between Amazon S3, RDS and EMR. Which service can help to process and move data between services?

1. Amazon Athena
2. Amazon QuickSight
3. AWS Data Pipeline

Answer: 3

Explanation:

> **1 is incorrect.** Amazon Athena is an interactive query service that makes it easy to analyze data in Amazon S3 using standard SQL

> **2 is incorrect.** Amazon QuickSight is a fast, cloud-powered business intelligence service that makes it easy to deliver insights to everyone in your organization

> **3 is correct.** AWS Data Pipeline is a web service that helps you reliably process and move data between different AWS compute and storage services, as well as on-premises data sources, at specified intervals

Question 2: Which service can be used to migrate an on-premises database to Amazon RDS?

1. AWS Server Migration Service
2. AWS Transfer for SMTP
3. Application Discovery Service
4. Database Migration Service

Answer: 4

Explanation:

> **1 is incorrect.** AWS Server Migration Service (SMS) is an agentless service for migrating on-premises workloads to AWS. However, for database migrations this is not the best service to use

> **2 is incorrect.** This service is not in scope for the exam but could turn up as a "distractor". Try to ensure you have a high-level understanding of all AWS services so you can easily eliminate distractors

> **3 is incorrect.** This service is not in scope for the exam but could turn up as a "distractor". Try to ensure you have a high-level understanding of all AWS services so you can easily eliminate distractors

> **4 is correct.** AWS DMS can be used to migrate an on-premises database to Amazon RDS

Question 3: Which service can be used to migrate exabytes of data into the AWS Cloud?

1. AWS Snowmobile
2. AWS Snowball

Answer: 1

Explanation:

    1 is correct. Snowmobile is "exabyte scale" with up to 100PB per Snowmobile

    2 is incorrect. Snowball is "petabyte scale"

Question 4: Which service can be used to migrate 50TB of data quickly and affordably to Amazon S3 for a company with a slow Internet connection?

    1. Amazon S3 Transfer Acceleration
    2. Amazon S3 multi-part upload
    3. AWS Snowball
    4. AWS Snowmobile

Answer: 3

Explanation:

    1 is incorrect. S3 Transfer Acceleration is used for fast uploads, but you do need a good connection and it does come at an extra cost

    2 is incorrect. S3 multi-part upload is good for breaking up large file for upload to S3. However, with 50TB of data over a slow connection it would be better to use AWS Snowball

    3 is correct. This is the best solution for this amount of data as the company has a slow connection

    4 is incorrect. AWS Snowball is overkill for this amount of data

Question 5: How can a company migrate a database from Amazon EC2 to RDS without downtime?

    1. Create an RDS read replica and then promote replica to master
    2. Create a new database from an EBS snapshot
    3. Migrate using the AWS Database Migration Service (DMS)

Answer: 3

Explanation:

    1 is incorrect. You cannot create an RDS read replica from a database running on EC2

    2 is incorrect. This would incur downtime as you have to launch a new database from the snapshot. You can't do this from EC2 to RDS either

    3 is correct. Context makes this one a bit easier! Just remember that DMS can migrate databases online without downtime and it supports many different source / destination options

Question 6: A company needs to migrate several TB of data from an on-premises NAS device to Amazon FSx. Which service can the company use to migrate the data over a VPN connection?

    1. AWS Database Migration Service (DMS)

2. AWS Snowball Edge
3. AWS DataSync
4. Amazon S3 Transfer Acceleration

Answer: 3

Explanation:

1 is incorrect. AWS DMS is used for migrating databases

2 is incorrect. Snowball Edge is used for migrating data using a physical device, not over a network

3 is correct. AWS DataSync can migrate data from on-premises NAS storage to Amazon S3, EFS, and FSx

4 is incorrect. S3 Transfer acceleration is used for improving upload speeds to S3. It does not migrate data to Amazon FSx

CONCLUSION

We trust that these training notes have helped you to gain a complete understanding of the facts you need to know to pass the AWS Certified Cloud Practitioner exam the first time.

The exam covers a broad set of technologies. It's vital to ensure you are armed with the knowledge to answer whatever questions come up in your certification exam. We recommend reviewing these training notes until you're confident in all areas.

BEFORE TAKING THE AWS EXAM

Familiarize yourself with the AWS platform

If you're new to Cloud Computing, it's highly advisable to take the instructor-led video course from Digital Cloud Training for a more detailed understanding of the AWS services before sitting your exam. With over 12 hours of video lessons, this on-demand video course will maximize your chances of passing your exam first time with a great score.

Assess your exam readiness with practice exams from Digital Cloud Training

These popular practice tests are the closest to the actual exam question format and the only exam-difficulty questions on the market. If you can pass these mock exams, you're well set to ace the real thing!

To learn more, visit https://digitalcloud.training/aws-certified-cloud-practitioner/

Challenge Labs

Learn by doing and gain practical, real-world cloud skills with our scenario-based hands-on exercises that run in a secure sandbox environment. Simply the best way to gain hands-on skills. To learn more, visit https://digitalcloud.training/hands-on-challenge-labs/

REACH OUT AND CONNECT

We want you to have a 5-star learning experience. If anything is not 100% to your liking, please email us at support@digitalcloud.training. We promise to address all questions and concerns. We really want you to get great value from these training resources.

The AWS platform is evolving quickly, and the exam tracks these changes with a typical lag of around 6 months. We are therefore reliant on student feedback to keep track of what is appearing in the exam. If there are any topics in your exam that weren't covered in our training resources, please provide us with feedback using this form https://digitalcloud.training/student-feedback. We appreciate your feedback that will help us further improve our AWS training resources.

To discuss any exam-specific questions you may have, please join our private Facebook group. It's a great space to ask questions and share knowledge and exam tips with the AWS community: https://www.facebook.com/groups/awscertificationqa

BONUS OFFER

To assess your AWS exam readiness, we have included one full-length practice exam from

Digital Cloud Training. These 65 exam-difficulty practice questions are timed and scored and simulate the real AWS exam experience. To gain access to your free practice exam on the interactive online exam simulator, visit https://digitalcloud.training/free-aws-practice-questions-cloud-practitioner/ or simply scan this QR code.

For those who have already purchased the full set of practice questions, please note that the 65 questions are included in the pool of 500 questions.

REQUEST YOUR FREE PDF VERSION

Based on the feedback we've received from our Amazon clients, we understand that studying complex diagrams in black and white or accessing reference links from a kindle device may NOT offer the best learning experience.

That's why we've decided to provide you with a PDF version at no additional charge. To access your free PDF version, simply send us a **screenshot of your review on Amazon** to CCPTNPDF@digitalcloud.training with **CCPTNPDF** in the subject line. You will then get FREE access to the PDF version within 48 hours. Should you encounter ANY problems with your review, please reach out. We're here to support you on your cloud journey.

LEAVE US A REVIEW

Your reviews help us improve our courses and help your fellow AWS students make the right choices. We celebrate every honest review and truly appreciate it. You can leave a review at any time by visiting amazon.com/ryp or your local amazon store (e.g. amazon.co.uk/ryp).

Best wishes for your AWS certification journey!

ON-DEMAND TRAINING, CHALLENGE LABS AND LIVE BOOTCAMPS FROM DIGITAL CLOUD TRAINING

At Digital Cloud Training, we offer a wide range of training courses that help students successfully prepare for their AWS Certification exams and beyond. Check out the range of training options below.

ON-DEMAND / SELF-PACED AWS TRAINING

Prepare for your next AWS certification with video courses & practice exams / exam simulator. We also offer training notes and practice tests in PDF format for offline study.

All of our on-demand courses are available on digitalcloud.training/aws-training-courses

With our Membership Program, you gain unlimited access to ALL of our on-demand courses – current and future – with early access to new content and updates. To get a taste, start your Monthly Membership or sign up for 12 months of unlimited access to our entire library of AWS training courses.

To learn more, visit https://digitalcloud.training/all-access/

CHALLENGE LABS

Keen to gain practical, real-world cloud skills? Then Challenge Labs are for you. Hone your skills across the most in-demand technologies, practice role-based cloud skills, and get the hands-on experience you need for certification exams.

Hands-on Challenge Labs are scenario-based exercises that run in a secure sandbox environment. These online scored labs offer extensive hands-on opportunities for all skill levels without the risk of cloud bills!

Ranging from fully guided to advanced hands-on exercises, Challenge Labs cater for all skill levels. At Digital Cloud Training we offer Challenge Labs for different levels of learners:

- **Guided** – Simply follow the step-by-step instructions in the guided labs with detailed hints to learn the fundamentals.
- **Advanced** – Create solutions according to requirements with supporting documentation – each step is checked / validated.
- **Expert** – Create solutions according to requirements with basic instructions and no supporting information – receive a final score.

Our Challenge Labs catalog includes over 1000 on-demand challenges across multiple cloud platforms and technologies including AWS, Azure, Docker, Linux, Microsoft, VMware and Cybersecurity.

To learn more, visit https://digitalcloud.training/hands-on-challenge-labs/

LIVE BOOTCAMPS (VIRTUAL CLASSROOM)

Get ready for your next cloud job with real-world projects in a virtual classroom.

AWS bootcamps are our most intensive training programs with live training sessions in a virtual classroom (via zoom).

The expert-led training sessions provide you with the opportunity to deep dive into AWS through real-world projects and hands-on exercises to help you develop practical experience.

Delivered by experienced AWS instructors, our cloud bootcamps will fully prepare you for your next AWS certification and a successful cloud career.

ABOUT THE AUTHOR

Neal Davis is the founder of <u>Digital Cloud Training</u>, AWS Cloud Solutions Architect and successful IT instructor. With more than 20 years of experience in the tech industry, Neal is a true expert in virtualization and cloud computing. His passion is to help others achieve career success by offering in-depth AWS certification training resources.

Neal started **Digital Cloud Training** to provide a variety of training resources for Amazon Web Services (AWS) certifications that represent a higher standard of quality than is otherwise available in the market.

Digital Cloud Training provides <u>AWS Certification exam preparation resources</u> including instructor-led Video Courses, guided Hands-on Labs, in-depth Training Notes, Exam-Cram lessons for quick revision, <u>Hands-on Challenge Labs</u> and exam-difficulty Practice Exams to assess your exam readiness.

With Digital Cloud Training, you get access to highly experienced staff who support you on your AWS Certification journey and help you elevate your career through achieving highly valuable certifications. Join the AWS Community of over 750,000 happy students that are currently enrolled in Digital Cloud Training courses.

CONNECT WITH NEAL ON SOCIAL MEDIA

All Links available on **https://digitalcloud.training/neal-davis**

 digitalcloud.training/neal-davis

 youtube.com/c/digitalcloudtraining

 facebook.com/digitalcloudtraining

 Twitter @**nealkdavis**

 linkedin.com/in/nealkdavis

 Instagram @**digitalcloudtraining**

Made in the USA
Columbia, SC
21 July 2023

ca9d3f29-4e63-41fc-8115-ca1d7e3810b0R01